R.D.BURMANIA
PANCHAMEMOIRS

Torrent of Compliments .....

* "Memoirs written by journalist Chaitanya Padukone on RD Burman.....well deserved" —**Amitabh Bachchan on Twitter (T-2300) and on his Face Book** – also posted an image of the front cover of the book.

* "Chaitanya, your affection and respect for Pancham is exemplary," —**Rishi Kapoor**

* "Besides his versatile repertoire , one also craves to know his 'true colours' as well. That's exactly why I enjoyed reading this entire book, as it truly describes Pancham-da, whose food was his music, with lots of interesting anecdotes from his life…—**Anup Jalota**– eminent devotional, classical and ghazal singer.

* "Being a music lover myself, I enjoyed reading every bit of this book that drifted me to the past. Was fascinated by some of the rarest photos of RDB with legendary actors; the most heart-wrenching photo is bereaved RDB sitting near his father Dada Burman's lifeless body. It was so heart-warming to read the eloquent tributes by Amitabh Bachchan, Sanjay Bhansali and Mahesh Bhatt." —**Devi Dutt**— producer of film 'Masoom' Filmfare award-winning music by RDB .and younger brother of legendary Guru Dutt.

* "Nicely composed thoughts & quotes brought alive beautifully on paper... I relived the cherished golden yesteryear memories!...God bless!"—**music director Pyarelal Sharma**—of legendary duo Laxmikant Pyarelal–and a close, dear friend of Panchamda.

* "Nonstop, I finished reading this engrossing book — as it is full of nostalgia... Grab it before it's sold out"—**Amod Mehra**—reputed Bollywood film and music critic and cine-trade analyst.

* "This book also provides rare valuable authentic insights into the 'X-entric' streak and the 'X-factor' of the genius behind the maestro musician mask" –**Kersi Lord and Ramesh Iyer** –acclaimed veteran ace musicians-arrangers who played for RDB's hundreds of chartbuster song-recordings.

* "Book Of The Year... The Definitive Biography by Chaitanya ! A lot has been said and heard about PANCHAM...through many books, but this is something different from others...keep it up"—**Rajesh 'Raj' Nagul**—Founder-member of **Team Panchammagic (Pune)** passionate RDB fans association.

* "The book is very interesting. For all RDB fans who wish to know the iconic composer up close & personal, this book 'R D BurMania' is a 'keepsake'. The anecdotes have been culled from Chaitanya's actual personal interactions with the legendary Panchamda." —**Anju Maskeri—Sunday Mid-Day**

* "Some of these episodes do make you understand the man even more than what you have been fed about him so far. Also, the book does well to take the reader into the life and times of R.D. Burman as the person, instead of his work as a musician. This is good because enough has been written, said and heard about his work."— '**Bollywood Hungama**' web portal.

* "It's an exhilarating chartbuster book that depicts R D Burman so candidly," —**Ananth Mahadevan**—popular actor, music-savvy prolific film-director who directed 'Dil Vil Pyar Vyaar'– a cinematic musical tribute to Panchamda!

R.D.BURMANIA
PANCHAMEMOIRS

CHAITANYA PADUKONE

Notion Press

Old No. 38, New No. 6
McNichols Road, Chetpet
Chennai - 600 031

First Published by Notion Press 2016
Copyright © Chaitanya Padukone 2016
All Rights Reserved.

ISBN 978-1-945579-85-1

Disclaimer

Chaitanya D. Padukone holds the moral right to be identified as the author of this memoirs-tribute work.

The views, opinions expressed by, as also the factual inputs shared with the author, by the various eminent celebrities and musicians featured in this book, are their own. The author and publishers are not in any way liable for the same.

The author wishes to express his reverential regards for the iconic composer-singer R D Burman and his vast awesome repertoire. At the same time, the author also places on record his earnest respect for the phenomenal talent of all the other legendary Bollywood composers, singers, lyricists, sound-recordists, music-biz magnates, as well as all the 'unsung heroes' of Indie film music fraternity.

Photo-Image courtesy/credits: Ashim Samanta, Asha Bhosle, Rishi Kapoor, Jatin (Satish) Wagle, Amit Kumar, Leena Chandavarkar-Ganguly, Barkha Roy, Devi Dutt, Poornima (Sushma Shreshta), Shyam Aurangabadkar, Jagdish Aurangabadkar, Chaitanya D. Padukone, Gajanan Mestry, Pyarelal R. Sharma, Anandji V. Shah, Trimurti Films (Rajiv G.Rai), Vimal Kumar, Navketan Films (Suneil Anand), B. K. Tambe, Viju A. Katkar, Vimal Kumar, Ranjit 'Kaancha' Gazmer, Kersi Lord, Burjor Lord, Shabbir Kumar, Umesh Chandra Malviya.

In the event that, the credit 'courtesy by-line' of any photographer, writer or the source, has inadvertently been un-credited or omitted we would be happy to include the same, on notification by the concerned individual/s in subsequent/future editions, if any.

Meticulous efforts have been put in to incorporate accurate data-facts and figures to the best extent possible. However, if any discrepancy or incorrect data has inadvertently crept in, the same would be rectified, on notification, in subsequent/future editions, if any.

Dedicated to

Both my parents, **late Devidas V. Padukone** and **late Kamala D. Padukone** — Whatever I have achieved in my career is all thanks to their blessings, their unconditional love and motivating support.

Every music lover and the legion of passionate **Pancham-*Premis* (across India and all NRIs)** who would love to step aboard a first-hand 'flight' journey of myriad *jhalaks* (glimpses) into the fascinating world of the maverick-genius composer-singer **R. D. Burman,** who was 'married to music.'

Amitabh Bachchan

March 27th, 2016

Legendary composer-singer R. D. BURMAN (Pancham-Da)

His name 'Pancham' signified his presence and personality. The musical note 'pancham' is difficult to reach in singing terms. Metaphorically then, his talent was way ahead of time and difficult to reach... RDB was modern and contemporary and yet never strayed away from the classical...that required genius.

Pancham-da thrived and excelled in times, when music compositions were 'unplugged.' When you think of that in today's 'plugged-in' times, you begin to understand and appreciate his mastery.

I was privileged and honoured to have sung 'playback' under his brilliant baton for this soulful composition in 'Mahaan' ('Jidhar dekhu teri tasveer') and also in 'Pukaar' for this peppy number 'Tu maike math jaiyyo.'

Amitabh Bachchan

Contents

Foreword

It may sound incredible, but as a schoolgoing kid, my music sense was crazily addicted to Pancham-da's songs, like the cult hippie number 'Dum maro dum' and 'Piya to ab toh aaja' and songs from 'Jawani Diwani,' which I would religiously hear on the radio. That RDB song track with the staccato tabla beats—'Jab andhera hota hai,' sung by Bhupinder-ji and Asha-ji—was my favourite fancy fixation. Whenever I would visit my rich cousin's house, who had a record player, I would refuse to have my dinner or let them eat unless I heard that number.

Right from my childhood and until now, I have worshipped my dearest composer RDB's marvelous work. Even this morning, before coming to my production office, I was listening to 'Yeh vaada raha.' Of course, as time passed, I also listened to classy compositions of the legendary Madan Mohan and Jaidev. But, honestly, with RDB's music, I imbibed the joy of listening to music.

It was like a godsend opportunity when I was asked to take charge of the 'songs' direction' of Vidhu Vinod Chopra's both movies 'Parinda' and '1942: A Love Story'—aka 'ALS'—because both had their music scored by RDB. Unfortunately, I had not met Pancham-da personally during the making of 'Parinda.' After all these years of my *"pancham tapasya"*, the D-Day finally dawned when I was asked to meet 'Dada' for the music sitting of '1942: ALS.' It was for me to understand the musical interpretation and also conceive the visuals. Finally I met Rahul-da, who was clad in a black silk kurta and a black silk lungi. Seeing him sit right in front of me was one of the most precious moments of my life in showbiz. At this music setting, I had the privilege to watch Pancham-da compose 'Ek ladki ko dekha toh aisa lagaa.'

It must have taken him hardly fifteen minutes to compose that entire song, along with the musical interludes that would adorn that masterpiece dhun. In keeping with his forte, for not conforming to norms, the song had no 'antara' and was a pure, simple 'period' melody. Defying conventional musical forms that were popular during those years, he dared to divert in the 'opposite' direction. With his glorious flow of talent, he did not have to make any effort to 'create'; it just came to him. And Dada seemed to celebrate that moment of ecstatic joy in his own discrete way. It was something very special that I got to learn from the modest maestro, who single-handedly revolutionized music in the Hindi film industry.

Then there was this classic waltz number 'Kucch na kaho,' the female version of which was rendered by Lata didi. Here, again, Lata didi is the other legend whom I worship and am always in awe of. When didi came for the song recording, it was yet another dream-fulfilled day for me—she even glanced at me. Even after two decades, she still remembers seeing me at the studio and watching her sing. But the studio atmosphere was charged with a numb sense of loss and grief, as Pancham-da was 'no more.' And as the lyrics 'Kucch na kaho' spelt out, we were all speechless for a while. But, as they say, the show had to go on.

While picturising the 'Kucch na kaho' song, a film producer, whom I do not wish to name, who visited the sets, had the audacity to scoff and say, 'Yeh 'lori' ko kaun sunega.' It was very disheartening. When '1942: ALS' was finally released, I had gone to watch 'Anjaam' on the first day in a theatre. Out there, I heard young boys in the stalls loudly humming that same song, which, ironically, that producer had mocked at, as a lullaby.

During all the song recordings, it was a huge learning experience just by observing the 'meticulous' Pancham-da at work. He used to brief singer Kavita Krishnamurthy with inputs as to how she should visualise a bee zooming to sting her and thus, with expression, sing the song 'O' Bhanwraa' in 'Pyar hua chupke se.' He also coached Kumar Sanu on the dynamics of voicing. Beyond the dulcet melodies and the pulsating yet soothing rhythm, Dada allowed 'space' for listeners to 'float' within.

When it comes to composing music for my own films—like for my last magnum opus 'Bajirao Mastani'—I retain my own distinct style. But subconsciously, I keep thinking, 'What if RDB had done it? How would he have executed it? How do I achieve the Pancham-wala level of chord progression, sound-balancing and mixing, like, for instance, when I recorded with Shreya Ghoshal?'

My fervent prayers were surely heard by 'someone up there' who likes me. Because that little boy who used to scurry towards the radio to listen to his favourite RDB chartbusters, he eventually met his music idol in person—and even got to direct the songs of his last movie! Having stood the test of time, Pancham-da's scintillating scores, which are inspired from deep within, will have their resonance over the next hundred years. *Hamesha goonjte hi rahenge.*

Wish you the very best, Chaitanya, for your 'R D BurMania–PanchaMemoirs'

– Sanjay Leela Bhansali

Author's Note

Dear ReaDers and Die-haRD Fans

'*Woh aa gaya, dekho woh aa gaya*' goes the ecstatic refrain in one of Pancham-da's sultry, sensuous iconic cabaret number 'Piya tu.' That lyrical phrase, I feel, applies to '**Rahul Dev-the Monarch of Melodies**' when he 'arrived' on the music horizon. **He came, he composed, he conquered**—the minds, thc hearts and the feet of both the young and old, when he unplugged his 'RD-X' brand, which radically redefined Hindi film music, where the 'X' stands for X-traordinary with the sporadic X-entric tinge.

The life and times of '**rebelutionary**' **composer-singer,** whose middle name is **Dev** (i.e., 'God' of Bollywood music), is like a massive ocean of sound waves: the deeper you dive, the more there is to explore. This Burmanesque book, which you will enjoy reading, relishing and ruminating on, is an earnest deviation from other exhaustive anthology-biographies. It's a unique treasure of **some** of my personal memoirs in a flashback mode, which **attempts** to delve into the 'Panchamystique' and unravel the '**the Real RDB.**'

As a film and film-music journalist and his aRDent fan, I shared a close personal rapport with the legendary **music maestro, Rahul Dev Burman** (*Pancham-da*), during his lifetime, for **ten years,** that is, from 1983 to 31 December 1993. Destiny was extra kind to me, as I have had the privilege of exclusively chatting with and **interviewing Pancham-da at song recordings and background recordings at Film Center (Tardeo, Mumbai).** That's because the press (print media) and visitors were **strictly prohibited** at RDB's studio recordings. Those days there was no electronic media, and digital media was unheard of. Besides meeting RDB at recordings, I also connected with him at dozens of film parties and movie premieres.

This is my honest, humble, authentic flashback recall of 'excerpts' from my personal meetings, encounters and interactions with R. D. Burman. The book attempts to string together amazing, amusing, and agonizing yet fascinating anecdotes, incidents and idiosyncrasies. As a bonus bonanza, I have included frothy tribute quotes from a galaxy of showbiz and music biz celebs, beginning with late superstar Rajesh Khanna, superstar Amitabh Bachchan, director Ramesh ('Sholay') Sippy, Lata Mangeshkar, Asha Bhosle, Randhir Kapoor, Rishi Kapoor, A. R. Rahman, Babul Supriyo, cricket maestro Sunil Gavaskar, Mahesh Bhatt, Zeenat Aman, Hema Malini, Jackie Shroff, Shekhar Kapur, legendary composers Pyarelal Sharma and Anandji Shah, 'Masoom' producer Devi Dutt (brother of the legendary Guru Dutt), producer Barkha Roy (of 'Sanam Teri Kasam'), Vidya Balan, Hariharan, Udit Narayan, Sonu Nigam, Himesh Reshammiya and so forth—all of whom I have personally interacted with. This book also features **candid and posed RDB pictures** clicked by me, besides an array of some **very rare, startling eloquent photographs** taken by veteran film press photographers. Incidentally, I am also a Western and Latin American rhythm player and would occasionally discuss intricate rhythm patterns with RDB, which is also one of the reasons I developed a close rapport with Pancham-da.

Over the years, I have been invited by various popular FM radio stations, including **Big FM, Radio One** and, of course, **Radio Mirchi,** where my interesting anecdotes were broadcast during RDB's anniversaries by the RJs to their respective loyal listeners. A number of Pancham Fan Clubs, live memorial concerts and Fan Associations, especially the enthusiastic **PanchaMMagic (Pune)** team, have also invited me as a guest of honour to share my nostalgic *"yaadon ki baaraat."* Invariably, the legendary composer's fans would surge towards me in large groups and inquire as to **when** I would chronicle some of my intriguing experiences in the form of a brief tribute book. In fact, even senior actors like the late superstar Rajesh Khanna (who was Rahul-da's close buddy) had often wondered aloud as to why I had never thought of coming out with my 'PanchaMemoirs.' It is pertinent to mention that a couple of biographies of R. D. Burman that have been launched in the recent past have 'reproduced' portions of paragraphs from my exclusive print-media interviews with the legendary composer-singer. Right from my very first meeting with RDB, I realized that he hated sycophancy and false flattery and preferred to be criticized for his flaws and faults. This facet of RDB has been dealt with in the initial chapters. Pancham-da would tell me, 'Both in sound recording and real life, it is essential to have balancing so that one remains always grounded.'

It was always an enlightening experience for me to interact with the genius known for his method-in-his-madness, who could breathe pulsating life into even the most insipid, inane lyrics or produce bizarre yet exotic sounds from mundane objects that would fascinate his fans and baffle rival composers, the bohemian who cared a damn both for marketing himself or for grabbing media attention. Money could never buy him—he survived and thrived mainly on world music.

Although iconic RDB may have passed away at an age of just fifty-four years, his legacy of hundreds of timeless chartbusters would keep his memories alive—possibly for the next 5400 years! The current relevance of RDB's hit retro tracks 'refrains' is evident these days in the titles of so many films and TV serials. Interestingly, the overture initial notes ending with the musical scat-scream 'Wakaao' has been cleverly recycled into 'Bachaao' as a signature theme in a popular insult-comedy TV show being telecast at prime time.

Ace drummer Franco Vaz regularly played for Pancham-da's 'takes,' and since I know him very well, I used to sit near him and watch him even as he played dexterously at RDB's recordings. Franco enthuses thus: 'Even after over two decades following Dada's untimely demise, hundreds of acoustic musicians—including me—singers and impresarios continue to earn decently out of RDB memorial concerts that are held quite often. The melody master's scores are indeed 'alive and everlasting,' he smiles.

What is terribly disheartening is that the maestro who conjured up such sterling scores had to suffer the ignominy of being ignored and being disowned by most of the showbiz industry. Where, if you are deemed no longer saleable, you are discarded, maybe like a used syringe.

On 27 June 1994, I somehow personally feel that the spirit of RDB has had a *"punar janam"* (rebirth) of sorts, because the same composer-singer who was rejected as a 'spent force' by showbiz steadily became such a sought-after phenomenal cult figure that his cynical detractors from the film fraternity had to swallow back their spewed venom and bow down to the film sangeet-supremo with apologetic reverence.

Unfortunately, the titan of Bollywood music was no longer there to witness this historical metamorphosis. But RDB lives on in the hearts of lakhs of all his loyal fans and retro music lovers like you.

Yours Musically,
Chaitanya Padukone

'Foodie' Pancham-da was passionate about growing highly pungent chillies (including the tiny yet tear-jerking z'ozio variety from West Indies) in the nursery garden below his building. Being a good cook, he would often use them in his own non-vegetarian recipes. Once when I asked him the 'mysterious' nexus between chillies and music, he replied, 'No teekha (spice) in the vocals and orchestration could make film music sound feeka (bland). Sooner or later you will realize the link between the two.' Six years after he passed away, when an FM radio station called 'Mirchi' came into being, one was left wondering if RDB was a 'soothsayer' as well! Incidentally, Pancham had specially composed a folksy 'laavani' number for 'Ashanti' (1982) sung by both Lata and Asha which goes 'Lavangi Mirchi'

PART 1

PANCHAMEMOIRS

1

Charismatic charm of cine-music: Sing is king

Aao jhoomein-gaayein, milke dhoom machaayein

'For me Hindi cinema is synonymous with melodious songs. They are as vital to the movies as, perhaps, fuel is to any car. They ignite the fantasy factor, flag off the recall value and accelerate the movie ahead. For that matter, I would never act in a movie which has no vibrant songs picturised on me,' said legendary thespian late actor-director **Dev Anand** when I quizzed him on the relevance of filmy songs. The agile Anand, it may be recalled, had declined the offer of the iconic 'angry young man' in Prakash Mehra's 'Zanjeer' only because there were no songs picturised on the hero. Of course, **Dev Anand's loss was Amitabh Bachchan's gain.** However, generally speaking, Bollywood cinema minus songs is like Alaska without snow or the United States devoid of fast-food culture or India sans the ubiquitous cricket craze. Film songs are inevitable catalysts that reign in every Indian's personal life. For every major 'situation' in our personal lives, there are nostalgic songs that each one relates to, be it romantic or melancholic, cultural or nuptial. Film composers would often be inspired by basic classical raagas or by rich regional folk music or even by Western jazz, rock, Arabic or Latino American rhythm beats. **From pioneers R. C. Boral and Pankaj Mullick to R. D. Burman, from Anil Biswas to A. R. Rahman, from Chitalkar Ramchandra** to Himesh Reshammiya and from Shankar Jaikishan to Shankar Mahadevan, the Hindi film song has undergone a spectrum of hummable harmonies. These were initially captured on primitive recording apparatus, which innovated to the analogue and then to digital and to today's hi-tech Dolby Atmos formats. Like modern touch-screen cell phones, songs too served as multipurpose. 'At times, one or two mediocre songs give the audience a breather, some sort of a musical relief, especially in a tense action-crime-drama-thriller movie. Or they can sneak out for a smoke or to rush to the toilet,' analysed composer R. D. Burman during his lifetime when I met him during recordings at Film Center. Film-makers love to launch the audiences into the orbit of tuneful 'dream sequences.' The late revered Raj Kapoor had an intriguing explanation for this when I met him on the sets of his 'Ram Teri Ganga Maili' at an erected pandal at Shivaji Park, Mumbai. He said, 'Songs are an escapism route for the common man, where, for three minutes, he takes off on a fantasy trip. What he cannot possibly behave in 'real life' in terms of romancing his beloved, the cine-goer derives that on-screen pleasure. It's an autohypnosis audio-visual trance, where the theatre audience identifies with the hero or heroine.' Indie cine-music history takes pride in the fact that one of the initial sound-talkie movies 'Indrasabha' (1932) consisted of a whopping number of nearly seventy-two songs (phew!), including dialogue verses, ghazals and thumris. It only goes to prove that the phenomenon of the 'songs syndrome' was ushered in by our 'enterprising' ancestors as if they had opened the 'musical floodgates' ever since the 'gaana khazaana' has been an integral part of the desi cinema culture. The music-savvy actor-director Manoj ('Bhaarat') Kumar, known for his movies with patriotic fervor, feels that film songs also play a cardinal role in promoting national integration. 'Very often, the entire theatre audiences comprising a diverse cross section of castes and communities are heard humming popular Hindi chartbuster songs either loudly in chorus or in low tones. The songs are the catalysts which unite our music-loving nation. For that matter, when my iconic retro movies 'Upkaar' and 'Purab Aur Paschim' were released, NRIs across the globe felt highly charged with patriotism as they recited and swayed to the sentiment-laden songs,' recalls Kumar when he spoke to me many years ago at a filmland party. The first-ever Bollywood superstar, **Rajesh Khanna,** was frank enough to share with me that besides his histrionic talents, he owes his super-stardom to a great extent to his dozens of chartbuster songs that made him the 'eternal romantic phenomenon.' **But in the successive superstar Amitabh Bachchan's case, there were no songs picturised on him in 'Anand,' 'Namak Haram,' 'Zanjeer' and 'Deewaar.'** No, the masses did not miss his doing a lip-sync to the songs—simply because they were unanimously in awe of the 'angry young man,' whose intense, volatile scenes and dialogues were the hallmark of those classic films. Current heart-throb superstar **Shah Rukh Khan,** known for his out-of-this-world blissful screen romance, where females go into a frenzy as he woos his heroines, opines that 'awesome songs ensure the repeat value and help elevate a film to a mega-hit status, provided the content is also gripping enough.' Not just the songs, but the background score too of every Hindi movie plays a vital role. Interestingly, the witty **Pancham-da (R. D. Burman)** once mentioned to me, that the background score is literally the 'unsung hero,' because it is mostly instrumental with occasional vocals or chorus. The 'Sholay' composer, the maverick Pancham-da (RDB), explains, 'The appropriate background music has the potent power to effectively drive an entire audience to collectively laugh, cry, be tense or be petrified, within a matter of five seconds. You don't hear. Rather, you actually 'feel' this blended music which enhances the visual impact. Try putting on zero volume, the **background music** in the dramatic fight-action scenes as in **'Deewar'** or the entire heart-rending death scene of Amitabh's character in that same landmark movie. Observe the dull, lacklustre impact. Or silence the build-up music in the pre-climax Shammi Kapoor scene, where he discovers the killer's identity in 'Teesri Manzil,' and watch how the otherwise gripping scene loses its chilling bite.' Composer-arranger-conductor **Pyarelal Sharma** (of the legendary **Laxmikant-Pyarelal** duo), who is hailed in music biz for his brilliant background scores, feels that 'both songs and background music complement each other in a movie.' Pyare-bhai enthuses, 'There are numerous movies where instrumental themes are repeatedly played and have a high recall value. Like, for instance, our haunting 'flute' theme in 'Hero' (1983) was recycled and remixed once again in 'Heropanti' (2015) after thirty-two years.' Veteran erudite composer **Anandji** (of legendary duo **Kalyanji-Anandji**) proclaims, 'What is not told on screen by the camera, nor by the actors, nor by any dialogues is effectively conveyed only through background music. Very often, chartbuster songs can contribute a great deal in boosting the 'long-run' box-office fortunes, like, for instance, our movies, including 'Don,' 'Zanjeer,' 'Qurbani' and 'Tridev,' he shrugs. Interestingly, Hollywood stars who visit India at film festivals or for other events seem to be in an 'enviable awe' of the Bollywood 'playback-song syndrome' and its vibrant screen picturisation. Stunning emergency physician-medico-cum-glam actress **Kalpana Pandit**, who is based out of Los Angeles, United States, discloses that some 'A-list' Hollywood stars whom she occasionally meets at premieres and after-parties are apparently 'fascinated by spectacular lip-sync movie-dance-songs in Indian movies,' as they feel it's something unique that they miss while watching English flicks. It may be safely surmised that Hindi movie songs may be deemed as 'Hollywood's envy, India's pride.'

—Chaitanya Padukone

Tailpiece: The suspense-thriller 'Hulchul' (1971), which marked the debut of Zeenat Aman, had 'no' songs at all. Instead, the experimental R. D. Burman has given a spectrum of only background instrumental "saaz aur aawaaz", humming the title 'Hulchul' even as he blends his own vocals and that of Asha Bhosle. When the credit titles are rolling, you get to see a potpourri of contrasting dance forms ranging from Japanese and Spanish to African tribal and classical Indian. In the same movie, Zeenie baby is seen swinging to a fast tempo 'soul beat' rhythm with Prem Chopra, making it look like a subtle precursor to 'Dum maro dum.' Incidentally 'Hare Rama Hare Krishna' also released in the same year 1971.

2

Punch-packed 'Pancham'—
The Real RDB

Author Chaitanya Padukone shares his memoirs.

Guru-Dev Burman - the PanchaMission

In the presence of megastars Amitabh Bachchan and Dilip Kumar, I was honoured with the prestigious Dadasaheb Phalke Academy Award in 2012, Mumbai, for 'three decades of dedicated devotion to film journalism'—**which I publicly dedicated to the fond memory of my 'guru' Pancham-da. Perhaps I am the only senior film scribe who considers legendary singer-composer Rahul Dev Burman as his mentor**, because, otherwise, there are thousands of eminent singers and musicians, globally, who look up to him as their inspiring icon or guru. But one has rarely heard of any journalist hailing RDB as his or her guru.

Almost my entire pocket money during my school and college days would be spent listening to RDB chartbusters. Instead of playing cricket with my buddies, I would be constantly inserting coins into 'jukebox' slots at various 'Irani' restaurants, known for their homely ambience, across South Mumbai. Left with no money to order for snacks and caramel, my appetizing starters were only the audible gems from Pancham-da's repertoire. But then, surprisingly, the restaurant manager-cashier would send me complimentary toast sandwiches.

Because, according to him, customers would end up ordering repeatedly for food and beverages as they would be under a 'spell,' enjoying the mesmerizing RDB-composed songs. That, then, was the chronic yet blissful **Panchamania** fever that I was down with.

Not surprisingly, my classmates sometimes called me 'junior RDB,' as I used to dexterously play Pancham-da's intricate rhythm patterns on Western rhythm instruments. My cherished aspiration was to meet my iconic figure, Pancham-da, someday, which I did, very briefly, when I bumped into him at a couple of film award functions and at the song recording of 'Kya hua tera vaada' at Film Center in 1977. But my bigger dream was to engage him in a lengthy conversation on his repertoire. But why would he get into a discussion with me? I was neither a top producer nor a director or a lyricist or a singer. That's how I kick-started on my journalistic '**PanchaMission.**'

Nahin nahin abhi nahin

Allow me to rewind into a snappy flashback. The legendary R. D. Burman, having completed twenty-five years in showbiz, had finally won his first-ever Filmfare Award for 'Sanam Teri Kasam.' All these years the honour was eluding him, as he was only being 'nominated' (over fifteen times!) but had never won it. There were whispers in showbiz circles that despite being declared the F/f award winner, RDB was secretly 'unhappy.' That's what intrigued me all the more. As a budding showbiz journalist in **July 1983,** when I first went to 'interview' him on two occasions at Film Center recording studio in Mumbai, he 'refused' to give me an interview! Because I made this advance confession to him that I was his ardent fan. But he had his logical funda in place. '**Come back again only as an unbiased music critic, not as my fan,**' he said in his stern yet friendly tone.

That was **my first 'guru mantra' from Pancham-da in film journalism.** It was an uphill task for me to transform myself overnight from a passionate Pancham fan to a hardcore critic. Not wanting to lose the golden opportunity, post-midnight I sat unto the wee hours and drafted all kinds of tricky, sticky questions, including 'prickly' ones on why he was unhappy with his very first Filmfare Award, his penchant for Western music plagiarism, and even why he had stopped recording songs with Asha Bhosle. There was a major risk that he would squirm and abruptly stop the interview and ask me to 'get lost.' But then the 'Boss' (that's what his team of musicians fondly called him) himself had given me the permission to be 'grilled.'

Saamne yeh kaun aaya

On the day the appointment was fixed, the weather was stormy and inclement. Non-stop heavy rains had flooded the low-lying areas across Mumbai. So I tried calling up Film Center to check if the RDB recording had been cancelled. The phone was jangling at the other end—with nobody picking up the receiver. With great difficulty, wading through the floods, I managed to reach Film Center, as my residence was just twenty minutes away. Skeptical thoughts lashed thru my mind whether the 'Boss' had managed to come.

As soon as I arrived on the floor, the **first 'darshan' I got was that of RDB himself standing on the corridor railings, gazing at the rain and humming some tune.** For the first fifteen seconds, I actually thought I was 'hallucinating.' Clad in a bright red-and-white checked shirt with folded sleeves, he was puffing away on his favorite brand 'State Express 555' cigarette. Before I could even react, he stormed, **'Welcome Mr. Critic. Today, the rains have supported you. Because, until all my main musicians don't come, I can't start the music rehearsals. We will have enough time till then. Since you are dripping wet, don't step into the chilled console-control room; you will catch a cold. Come sit on the sofa, inside the other glass cabin where the AC is not working. I will instruct the canteen boy to get you a cup of** garam chaai, **you will feel better,'** he ushered me into a comfort-zone, as he continued smoking. Few minutes later he joined me. It was pre-decided by **RDB's** manager-secretary, **Bharat Ashar, that we would chat only for about twenty minutes. But then the animated discussion became so engrossing that it went on for nearly '120 minutes.'**

Contrary to what I had expected, Pancham-da faced all the prickly questions with an air of modesty and honesty. Apparently, he also seemed to be impressed with my knowledge of various Latin-American rhythms, including the 'bossa nova,' which was among his favorites. **Intermittently, he would ask me to switch off my tape recorder when he wished to use 'abusive' language or react candidly which was 'not' for being published. Even as he was speaking to me, his subconscious 'stereophonic' mind was ticking away on some violin symphony, to be played for the background score.**

What touched me and swept me off my feet was his humility. After we finished the semi-marathon interview, he said, 'Listen, Mr. Padukone, my English is okay, but not all that good, because I am a high-school dropout. My musical grammar they all say is terrific, but my English grammar is below the mark. So wherever I have slipped up, *thoda dhyaan rakhna*. Overall, *vaise, maine jo bhi bola, theek bolaa naa?*' Then came the partying shot that almost knocked me out. 'The day I start giving you *'gaalis'* (abusive slang), it means I treat you as my friend. It will happen very soon,' he assured me as he patted me on my right shoulder.

Main tasveer utaarta hoon

Although I was clicking candid b/w pictures of RDB as he kept replying with animated gestures to my questions, it was not enough during the interview. As soon as the conversation was over, I also requested Pancham-da to pose on the keyboards and on a set of tympani drums, metallic maadal drums and against the grand piano as well. But he stipulated a condition:**'Please don't publish my candid pictures playing these musical instruments. Normally I sit with the harmonium at settings and studio rehearsals. *Mujhe thodi si acting karni padegi* posing on the synthesizers and drums. Let me sit at the massive mixing and balancing console in the Film Center control room. You, ideally, publish that picture,' he requested.** No prizes for guessing that I complied with his gentle command.

Little did Rahul-da know then, that three decades later, the same colour picture of RDB posing on the keyboards, clicked by me, would be used on the commemorative special postage stamp issued by the postal authorities.

Samay ka ye pal—thamsa gaya hai

Two weeks later, this interview with RDB was published in a leading English tabloid newspaper ('Mid-Day') in Mumbai. Two days later, I received a call. My dad picked up the landline receiver, as I was having my breakfast. 'There is some person on the line who says that R. D. Burman wishes to speak to you.' It was a rattling bolt from the blue— it took me twenty seconds to realize what my dad said. It was too incredible to be true. As I took the receiver in my hands, my heart skipped a few beats and was thumping. **Time stood still. Imagine getting a telecall from the musical icon whom you always idolized. The anxiety was double, because I was not too sure whether he was peeved, irked or pleased.** *"Hello, Padukone! Array, baba, kya likh diya tumne! Puraa pol khol diya,"* **he said in a furious tone and waited for my reaction. In an apologetic and quivering voice and amid mild palpitations, I said, 'Dada, I don't mind carrying clarifications, if you so wish.' There was hushed silence for ten seconds.**

Suddenly there was a chuckling laughter at the other end and RDB said, *'Itna tension mein aa gaya,* relax, I was just joking. You have written very well, and I already got over thirty calls from top film directors and singers, all of them appreciating the interview. In future, you definitely have the potential to be an award-winning writer. We must be in touch. *Milte hain,'* he insisted as he disconnected. It took me a good thirty minutes to reconcile that the same genius composer, whom I revered, had actually called me and complimented me. That whole day I was dazed. It was too good to be true.

Had Pancham-da been alive today and heard about my Phalke Award, he would have reacted with *"Yeh toh hona hi tha!."* Yet another cherry on the cake was that he had started peppering me with friendly *'gaalis'* when I frequently met him at song recordings and film parties.

Despite the major age difference, he had considered me to be a worthy 'young friend.' And I was even made a butt of his pranks at recordings and parties, once in a while.

'My fans are my rewards'

Almost every year, RDB's films would figure in the Filmfare Awards nominations for 'Best Music Director.' Often, there would be two nominations of Pancham-da's films, like in 1976, both 'Sholay' and 'Khel Khel Mein' were 'competing' with each other, but neither of them won. For that matter, in 1975, the year which Sachin-da passed away, RDB was pitted against his own maestro father's scores when 'Prem Nagar' and 'Aap Ki Kasam' were nominated. But neither of them could secure the coveted award.

The sensitive RDB would be disheartened when the awards would 'elude' him. On an optimistic note, he shared with me his reaction, with a tinge of emotion in his voice: 'When I really lost all hopes, I consoled and reminded myself that what is more important is 'rewards' and not 'awards.' My fans are my 'rewards.' But when I got my first Filmfare Award in 1983, I had also fulfilled my father Sachin-da's dream. That night I wept with joy.'

Why Pancham-da 'hated' composing cabaret numbers

As is a known fact, despite being a 'versatile' composer, R. D. Burman was and is predominantly known for his some two dozen racy Westernized cabaret songs (what is popularly tagged these days as 'item songs' in contemporary filmy jargon), like 'Piya tu ab to aaja' (Caravan), 'Aao na gale lagao na' (Mere Jeevan Saathi), 'Aaj ki raat koi' (Anamika), 'Shabnam naam hai mera' (Kati Patang), 'Meri jaan maine kahaa' (The Train), 'Aaja o mere raja' (Apna Desh), 'Mehbooba mehbooba' (Sholay) and many more. These songs have striking vocal gimmicks and intricate rhythm patterns besides, of course, the catchy melody. When I shared with RDB that his fans go into a frenzy while enjoying his awesome cabaret songs in the theatre, he gave me that 'Haan mujhe pataa hai' look.

But then he dropped his bombshell. Pancham-da stormed. 'It's a fact that the masses get turned on, as the songs also have seductive glamour-repeat visual value. But, honestly, at times, I hate composing cabaret songs because there is no soulful melody or inspiring lyrics in it. Whenever I compose raga-based melodies, I derive total creative satisfaction. Classical music is my forte,' he said nonchalantly, gesticulating with his left-hand fist.

When the thumri-based raga song 'Hume tumse pyar kitna' composed by RDB and sung by Begum Parveen Sultana merited a Filmfare Award, it was a loud testimony to all those who doubted his ability to conjure up classical numbers. This explains why RDB was not all that exhilarated when he won his first-ever Filmfare Award trophy for Best Music Score in 1983, which had eluded him for over two decades. **Off the record, he mentioned to me that since the movie 'Sanam Teri Kasam' had only a jazzmatazz Westernized score and no classical songs, he was disheartened. 'All these years, I expected the award for movies like 'Parichay,' 'Amar Prem,' 'Aandhi,' 'Kinaara,' 'Khushboo,' 'Mehbooba' and, of course, 'Kudrat,' all of which had situations for raga-based songs. But it was a series of 'miscarriages,''** he lamented. But some divine power above seems to have heard his grousing. When Pancham-da won his second consecutive Filmfare Award for producer Devi Dutt's 'Masoom,' that too in the same year 1983, he was delighted. Because this time there were three soul-stirring classical songs, especially the RDB composition 'Do naina aur ek kahani' which fetched the National Award and the Filmfare Award for the mellifluous singer Arati Mukherjee.

'Disco music is a passing fad'

Although RDB had composed disco-theme songs for movies like 'Sanam Teri Kasam,' 'Aamne Saamne,' 'Rocky' and even 'Jawani Diwani,' he was not particularly fascinated with that genre. When I quizzed him, he said, 'It's only because the situation warranted a disco kind of rhythm metre that I am compelled to compose. But I have tried to infuse wonderful melodies in such songs as in 'Saamne ye kaun aaaya,' 'Nisha-jaane-jaan,' and 'Aa dekhe zaraa,' for instance. Mostly, there is a loss of lyrical value, because the emphasis is more on the dance-based heavy-bass thumping rhythm. The disco songs which are played mainly in discotheques or pubs have definitely added a new dimension to film music. But they cannot last eternally like the evergreen immortal melodious hits. It's a passing fad.'

The 'raaz' behind RDB's evergreen repertoire

What was Pancham-da's raaz at composing soulful or rocking songs and singing some of them which emerge reigning evergreen chartbusters? After a deep drag on his favourite State Express 555 cigarette, RDB came up with his candid outburst. '**Being the son of maestro legendary composer Sachin-da (S. D. Burman) was initially a mixed blessing for me. That's because in Hindi film music history, unfortunately, I don't think any of the sons of any iconic music director or playback singer have surpassed their father's glorious success—or even come anywhere close to it.**' He paused and inhaled a puff on his cigarette. Was there any guru mantra which his 'Baba,' Sachin-da, had passed on to him? '**Be different from the rest. Carve your own distinct identity. If you are not different, the music lovers will be indifferent. Compose as many catchy tunes which are easily hummable or can ideally be whistled by the common layman when they cannot recall the lyrics'was my dad Sachin-da's precious advice to me.**

'That was when I started off with movies like 'Chhote Nawaab' and 'Bhoot Bungla' way back in the '60s.'RDB then continued, saying, 'Besides keeping frequent tabs on global trends in music and infusing latest foreign instrumental influences and unconventional sound effects in some of my Western songs, like the numbers from 'Jawani Diwani' and 'Hum Kisi Se Kum Nahin.' I would also try and ensure that most of my songs had simple lyrics, like 'Mere saamnewali khidki mein' from 'Padosan' or 'Yeh shaam mastaani' from 'Kati Patang' and foot-tapping melodies like 'Hum dono do premi' (Ajnabee). Most of my songs have either the swinging 'dance' factor like 'Ek main aur ek tu' (Khel Khel Mein) or the soulful 'haunting quality' of 'Dum maro dum' (Hare Rama Hare Krishna). Quite often, to grab the listeners' attention, I would use hoarse shrieks or chorus screams as in the prelude of songs like 'Duniya mein' ('Apna Desh') and 'Lekar hum deewana dil' ('Yaadon Ki Baarat') or 'Dekha na hai re' ('Bombay To Goa'). In living up to my nickname 'Pancham,' I would add my creative maverick 'punch' and try to make the song a 'smash hit' with the masses.

'My favourite mascot was the 'echo effect' like 'Ta Ra Ta Ra Ta Ra' in dozens of my songs, which is like my audio autograph. Right from my second film song 'Pyar karta jaa' (Bhoot Bungla, 1965), I had started using the echo effects with the help of Kersi Lord, and the effects fascinate me. The echo is also a symbol of 'resilience,' as the sound bounces back.

'A lot also depended on whether the film-maker was music-savvy and shared a tuneful rapport with me. Or whether the subject and situations were inspiring enough,' insisted the affable composer, who felt that every song was like a 'fusion of background score and choreography, because even before the track is recorded, the director explains in advance the whole scenario, the shot division, the camera movement, the action, and facial expressions of the actors.'

'Chura liya' hai tumne jo 'dhun' ko

Jestfully speaking Was 'copyright' redefined as the right to copy?

Although RDB was an acclaimed genius and was hailed in showbiz for composing instant original tunes, he would quite often get influenced by foreign tracks, some of which were cleverly adapted to the filmi Indie-pop patterns. Initially, the adventurous Burman Jr. would drop in to his teammate ace musician Kersi Lord's house and listen extensively to world music on vinyl LP discs. Years later, RDB would travel overseas extensively either for his shows or on vacation, and he would pick up audio cassettes of foreign musicians which intrigued him. Or he would diligently listen and make mental notes of live music concerts played at nightclubs.

There were these cynical detractors who felt that Pancham was a smart 'copycat' and openly 'lifted' foreign tunes. Since RDB had given me the 'blanket permission' to shoot any unpleasant question, I quizzed him about his being accused of plagiarism. Was 'copyright' redefined by him as the right to copy? This time, before responding to my question, he had three sips of lukewarm masala tea from a glass— he used to add water to make the steaming hot tea 'sippable.'

RDB said, 'In any creative profession, you cannot work in a mental vacuum. As far as Western songs, I have been inspired by just the first one, two or three or four hook-lines or the initial five bars, but the 'antaraa' and the rest is all my own. Like in 'Chura liya hai tumne' and 'Mehbooba mehbooba' and in 'Jab andhera hota hai.' And I have no complex in admitting this. Sometimes, it's the director who may insist that I adapt a particular foreign tune, as it happened in the case of 'Mehbooba mehbooba', he shrugged. With a penchant for listening to and watching Western rock star musicians, Pancham-da had his top favourites. 'There are so many Western composers I derive inspiration from. But the Jamaican–American composer-singer, Harry Belafonte, and the background title tracks of James Bond movies are my favourites. The staccato style of punctuating my songs with the vocal overtures 'Heh heh heh' is inspired by Belafonte. Even the guitar-flanger overlap effect in 'Dhanno ki aankhon mein' has been inspired by Belafonte's 'Merci Bon Dieu,'' he told me in a whisper. 'Then I love to listen to Antonio Carlos Jobim, the Brazilian master musician-singer, who pioneered the 'bossa nova,' followed by tracks of Sergio Mendez, yet another terrific Brazilian musician.'

What were his observations on the international scene? 'When I visited San Francisco,I met the foreign musicians out there. They told me that they would love to 'adapt' Indian classical melodies to their style. There is so much euphonic melody in Hindustani classical—they told me. There there is a Far East country group which has 'copied' the melodies of 'Aradhana,' I have that L.P. record.' he said and shrugged.

There was a valid counter justification that he also shared. 'On the flip side, I feel it's a boon for Indian music lovers so that they get to savour the 'world music' flavours of rock'n roll, jazz, cha-cha-cha, flamenco, calypso, santana, soul, bossa nova and waltz even as they are listening to hamare apne Hindi songs. Like in 'Oh haseena zulfonwaale' ('Teesri Manzil'), Shammi Kapoor fans would be actually swinging to 'rock'n roll' even as they are humming the song,' he analyses. 'But I have always tried as far as possible to be original and maintain my signature style. If you have observed, ethnic Nepali, Bengali and North Indian folk music has often influenced me, as is evident in 'Hogaa tumse pyara kaun' ('Zamaane Ko Dikhaana Hai') Or in 'Jai jai shiv shankar' ('Aap Ki Kasam'). For that matter, all classical songs are essentially derived from raagas, but sometimes I have tried to deviate from the *bandish*,' he countered. 'But whether it's classical or Western, I have always tried as far as possible to be original and maintain my unique style with my peculiar signature sounds. That's how my fans and music lovers are able to instantly identify my songs, which all have 'my audio autograph.'" He nods his head, peering through his geek glasses.

Meri (anokhi) aawaaz hi pehchaan hai

Unlike his father Sachin-da, known for his haunting nasal-timbre vocals like 'Mere saajan hai uss paar' (Bandini) or 'Kaaheko royye' (Aradhana), son RD consciously avoided singing classical songs, preferring to stick mainly to the high octave notes as in 'Mehbooba mehbooba' ('Sholay') or the rasp, grating tones as in 'Duniya mein' ('Apna Desh'). Why was it that Pancham-da rarely sang like a normal playback singer? There was a logical funda behind his bizarre scales. When asked, Pancham-da explained, 'Actually I have sung numerous Bengali film and non-filmy songs and various Hindi songs like Sharaabi Aankhen ('Madhosh') or Samundar Mein Nahake ('Pukaar') in my normal voice. Once again, my composer-singer father, Sachin-da, had earlier warned me that if I did not develop my own distinguished identity as an 'exceptional singer,' it would be very difficult to step out of his massive 'shadow.' The sons of almost all legendary singers and composers face this phenomenal problem. Moreover, I had a tonsils operation, during my childhood, which changed my tonal quality. My high-pitched octave ('Mehbooba mehbooba') and my grated, rasp vocals as in 'Duniya mein' (Apna Desh) blended with the breathing-gasping sounds gave me my unique identity as an 'unconventional and different' playback singer. And my songs, I am told, have emerged as chartbusters,' he says, with a mild blush flushing on his cheeks. During his life span, as an unconventional 'playback' voice, RDB sang some 36 'duets' with female singers and around 40 'solo' songs!

Would RDB throw light on what made him *gaao-chillao* in that grating, grunting voice? After a bout of chuckles, he pauses to light his cigarette, which he had forgotten. Typical of his absent-minded trait, whenever he was engrossed in a music session or in an interesting conversation. 'Hmm, it was the legendary Afro-American singer-trumpet player, Louis Daniel Armstrong, who had influenced me with his rasp, grating style of singing, which I had first experimented in 'Meri jaan maine kahaa' (The Train),' disclosed Pancham-da, who also secretly admired 'jazz-waltz' wizard composer, Jaikishan Panchal (of Shankar Jaikishen fame), the fusion-genius C. Ramchandra, virtuoso Salil Chaudhary and, of course, legendary Ghazal Badshah, Madan Mohan. With a fascination for listening to and watching Western rock star musicians, Pancham-da had his own personal top foreign musician favourites as disclosed in the preceding paragraphs.

Wasn't it true that RDB was almost supposed to sing a track in Marathi for the first time? 'The producer Satish Wagle being my buddy, I was being coaxed to sing the title song of this Marathi TV serial 'Yaala Jeevan Aise Naav' in my high-pitched voice, by its director, Anil Baindur. But I declined. Especially since I did not wish to cut a sorry figure with any wrong Marathi pronunciation. Ultimately, I got the eminent singer Chandrashekhar Gadgil (from Pune) to sing that Marathi track.' he smiled.

RDB was confident he would emerge the 'BMC'

Just eleven days before he passed away, I met Pancham-da at the release event of singer Amit Kumar's non-filmy album 'Mad,' where composer RDB was the 'chief guest'. The event had a relatively low media attendance. The event was convened by the record company and held on the terrace of a drab industrial gala building in the Saki Naka area in Andheri East (Mumbai suburb). So delighted was Pancham-da to see me that he tightly hugged me. It was a nasty twist of fate that even in showbiz print media, RDB was apparently considered 'no longer saleable.'

Coincidentally, on that same evening, a 'showman' film-maker had hosted his star-studded party at a '5-star hotel' elsewhere. Looking quite pale, Pancham-da had wrapped a woollen muffler around his neck, as he told me that he was recovering from malaria. For this other 'showman's party,' for obvious reasons RDB was 'not invited.'

An hour later, we were leaving from Amit Kumar's event. The *'bade dilwale'*Pancham-da asked his driver Ramesh to shift to the back seat, insisting on driving himself, and dropped me in his modest Fiat car at the other 5-star party venue. In a jolly mood, he commented on his car registration number: **'BMC 1139.' In a lighter vein, RDB stated that 'it stands for Best Music Composer.'** But I could sense traces in his voice that indicated **'I mean it.'** Before we said goodbye, Dada hummed two lines of the song 'Ek ladki ko dekha.' He enlightened me, saying, **'This song is unique because it has a long, winding 'mukhdaa' but no 'antaraa.' My dad, Sachin-da, has been mentoring me from above, and I will make him proud this time with the period music of the forties' decade.** *Pataa nahin,* **I have this gut feeling that I will regain my lost glory as a 'BMC' next year with '1942: A Love Story."**He sounded so optimistic. **RDB gave me a warm handshake for at least two minutes and then said, 'Let's celebrate my comeback with a bang in January 1994.'** As usual, he uttered his patented phrase "*millte hain.*" In turn, I responded with my usual phrase, also the title of his hit movie, 'yeh vaada rahaa.' But cruel destiny had other plans for the *sangeetkaar* par excellence. The supreme singer who had given us 'breathtaking' songs had abruptly breathed his last, during the wee hours of 4 January 1994, leaving behind his legacy of hundreds of 'children'—all his superhit songs; yes, they were like his brilliant babies, because Pancham-da himself had once told me that he was also 'married to his music.'

3

"Kuch bhi ho lekin mazaa aa gaya 'merry' jaan"

Partying shots

As a film-journalist-columnist attached a leading Mumbai-centric tabloid newspaper since 1983, I was invited to almost all the major **filmy parties** in Bollywood. The showbiz parties would be hosted in '5-star' hotels, frequently, at the drop of a hat—movie *'mahurat'* launching, music release, post-premieres, 100 days, silver and golden jubilees and, of course, birthdays of stars (whew!). Of the hundreds of 'bashes' that I attended, let me glide on to a flashback and recall just a **few interesting ones** that have remained etched on my mental 'memory card.' The icing on the 'party cake' would be that wherever the movie music score was by **R. D. Burman**, I would mostly get to meet up with him and briefly chat with him. But not everytime. Funnily, my very first music launch party, where I made my party debut, RDB was 'missing.' **Let's unwind into the 'rewind' mode.**

Why were Rajesh Khanna and Pancham both 'missing' at the 'Agar Tum Na Hote' party?

It was the musical milestone movie 'Agar Tum Na Hote' music-release occasion at the Searock Hotel (Bandra, Western suburb in Mumbai). The celeb guests, including lead cast Raj Babbar and scene stealer Rekha, were circulating around. But there was no sign of the superstar hero Rajesh Khanna and his buddy Pancham-da. Ravishing Rekha was praising RDB for having patiently 'mentored' her as a singer. Eventually the album was released in the 'absence' of both Kaka-ji (Khanna) and composer RDB. But what was the strange logic was what I was trying to figure out. That's when affable co-producer, Vimal Kumar, confided in me that it was a blunder on the part of the music company. 'They had changed the dates and suddenly convened the event without confirming the availability of RDB (who was not in town) and Khanna who was shooting on an overseas location,' revealed Vimal-ji discreetly. But the modest RDB was not someone who would be incensed about 'how dare they release the music minus me.' "*Gaane hit ho jaane chaiye, aur film chalni chahiye. Agar by chance hum naa bhi ho, toh show must go on*" was what self-effacing RDB told the producer when he went to specially meet him after he returned to the city.

'Jawaani' completion party

Peete hain shaan se

Yet another film party to celebrate the music release was that of this movie 'Jawaani' produced by the exuberant Ramesh Behl, who was an excellent host. This party, where the Scotch whisky was flowing, was held at the Searock Hotel but in an open-air terrace. RDB was on home ground because Behl was his close buddy. The film 'Jawaani' introduced Karan Shah opposite this Hong Kong-based NRI girl, Neelam Kothari. 'Do you understand the Hindi lyrics of the foot-tapping songs which for you have done lip-sync in this movie,' Pancham was overheard asking Neelam.

'Yes, I was told the gist of the lyrics, whilst shooting, but now I don't remember,' she chirped in Cantonese accent.

That's when RDB tried to make her comfortable. 'Don't worry, even I don't understand much of high-flown Hindi. So we are sailing in the same motor boat. You have an amazing star quality, and you will sign on many more movies,'he confidently predicted after he learnt that she was also a trained jazz-ballet dancer. That was when Neelam shrugged and drawled that she wanted to do maybe 'just one movie,' while she was on a vacation trip in Bombay (now Mumbai) and return to Hong Kong. As the party continued well past midnight, RDB wanted to leave, as he had some morning 'music sitting' the next day. But host Ramesh who was in a 'spirited' mood refused to let his buddy Pancham leave the party and clutched him tight. That's when RDB told him, 'One-for-the- road ek peg *lekar aata hoon*'. Instead of heading towards the cocktail bar, he discreetly sneaked out and, from a distance, gestured to me that he would be getting into his car literally on the road! That then was an impish facet of Pancham.

Two more parties at Searock this time. This catalyst monumental hotel, which was a mute witness to dozens of **Pancham-da music launches,** at land's end bandstand Bandra, today stands 'demolished.' Today, there is no *naam-o-nishaan* of this iconic hotel, which was also targeted by alleged terrorist attacks. There was a time when RDB used to jokingly 'rag' us that journalists should rent out an overnight 'tent-on-the-rocks' near the hotel, as after the frequent late-night parties, we had to return all the way home.

'Zameen Aasmaan' album release

"Jitni bhi taareef karo, main zameen par hi atkaa rahoonga," said RDB. It was the music launch of this Sanjay Dutt starrer 'Zameen Aasmaan' music release, where RDB was being profusely complimented for this awesome fusion raga-based Lata Mangeshkar number 'Aisa samaa na hotaa,' when it was played for the invited guests and the press. Now when this duet cabaret situation song 'Pyar naghma hai' was played, RDB was quietly standing in a corner and judging the reactions. *"Jinnko hamara-wala gaana achha lagaa, sirf unko khaana* (dinner) *milega,"* he said jestfully with a mock-frown. That's because Pancham had sung the fast-paced song in his normal voice minus any gimmickry. Initially, most of the invited guests had not realized that RDB had sung the song.

'Tum Karo Vaada' party

When RDB's pet had to see the 'vet'

The party to launch the music tracks of 'Tum Karo Vaada' (1993), which has singer Anaida (Raadhika) playing the female lead, had a sudden twist in the tale. That's because Pancham-da had to abruptly and discreetly exit from the small banquet hall at the Searock Hotel. The director, Robin Khosla, whispered that apparently RDB's pet dog was very sick which compelled him to rush home to arrange for emergency 'vet' treatment. Now what is noteworthy here is that being an 'animal lover,' RDB did not feel it necessary to hanker after grabbing media mileage. So attached was Pancham with his pet that he gave it priority over getting press publicity from being in the party. Of course, the party continued, but RDB's conspicuous absence was felt, as he was the 'cardinal star' that evening. That's because the cast comprised of relatively new debutants. How many such instances of self-exclusion from media glare do we find in today's times?

The 'Pantera' album release

Zamane ko dikhana hai—Pancham kisi se kam nahin

In keeping with his flair for the innovative, Pancham-da co-hosted the 'Pantera' (his non-filmi Latino album) party which had its trailer video clips screenings of the songs at the exotic 'Cavern' disco club near the Searock poolside. The atmosphere there was dark with psychedelic flickering dazzling lights. When I reached there, I could not spot RDB anywhere, and I presumed that the boss co-host had not yet arrived on the scene and would arrive fashionably late. It proved a wrong conjecture from my side. Just as I was about to be seated, suddenly two hands clutched me from behind, and the growly voice said, 'You are now caught in the panther's den. Grrrr!' Of course, I surmised it had to be RDB because I could recognize his hands or, rather, palms. Withdrawing his hands, he hugged me and said, 'Thanks, Padukone.' *"Tum time pey aa gaye.* Now feel at home. *Yeh apni hi party hai aur jaldi nikal mat jaana."* (*Observe his child-like quality and his being so down-to-earth*). After five repeat screenings of the video clips (*there was an encore demand*), the guests were all asked to come over to the banquet hall. There were large posters and cutouts of Pancham-da holding the guitar with a panther staring at him. Most of his buddy-producers and directors were all there, but the cynosure of all eyes was on Shammi Kapoor, who was the chief guest on the occasion. The late-evening party progressed, and it was probably past eleven. Being fairly new and having heard of Shammi-ji's rumoured reputation of being either curt or courteous at times, I was not hesitant to go and introduce myself. As if RDB had read my mind, he once again came from behind and asked me, "*Kya Shammi-ji se miloge nahin kya?*"

I fumbled and said, "*Uh uh haan, kyun nahin!*" In the next ninety seconds, I was facing the legendary Shammi Kapoor, with RDB only introducing me and vanishing from there, as there were other guests waiting to exchange pleasantries with him at the party. Sensing my nervousness, Shammi-ji broke the ice by saying, '*Beta*, besides RDB's Hindi songs, do you also listen to Latin American music? Because that will help you to appreciate the 'Pantera' tracks much better.' I nodded my head and informed him that sometimes whenever I visit my Goan friends, they play a few Latino LPs and cassettes and that I have heard Daniela Romo and tracks from the 'Santana' American Latin rock band.

That's when the 'Teesri Manzil' rock star stormed in his gruffy tones, 'No wonder Pancham has invited you. Keep listening. Not many music lovers in India relate to Latin–American music. In this movie 'Ek Se Bhale Do,' Pancham has playbacked for me in this song 'Lapa changa mein nache,' and I am merrily dancing to Latin–American rhythm beats.' Saying so the hefty Kapoor chuckled. Apparently, at the 'Pantera' party itself, whispers reached RDB's ears—the 'inside info' that his Latino overture was getting a lukewarm response at music stores. Most RDB addicts who were used to the particular Burman-brand were finding it tough to relate to the 'alien *dhun*.' In this venture, RDB's unintentional gaffe perhaps was that he was far ahead of his time. But all the same, he had fulfilled his mission of proving to the Latin–Americans that *"pancham kisi se kam nahin!"* When I went to bid goodbye to him, RDB clutched my hand tight but wore that 'anxious, disturbed look,' which speaks for itself.

The Jai Shiv Shanker completion party.

Kuchh bhi ho lekin mazaa aa gaya 'merry' jaan

The **'Jai Shiv Shanker'** movie completion 'informal' party was convened at Rajesh Khanna's office-cum-resting penthouse spacious terrace in Giri Raj building on Linking Road (Bandra-Khar in Mumbai). Being a bit of a 'recluse' when it came to celebrating with his very close buddies, Kaka-ji (Khanna, that is) very rarely threw open his Mexican-style cocktail bar. Thanks to the Latino–American décor, when RDB arrived, he was totally 'at home.' 'Welcome, Pancham, instead of the usual 5-star hotels, we are all meeting at a 'nil-star' venue.' Kaka-ji winked as he proclaimed loudly.

Instantly, RDB replied, *"Kaun kehta hai there are no stars. Yahaan neeche 'superstar' hain, aur aasmaan mein five hundred stars nazar aa rahe hain.* Cheers to that!" He then chuckled, after which he sat rotating on the cocktail barstool.

Incidentally, the Khanna was holding his corner 'durbar,' and everyone went up to him to exchange greetings. When I went up to him, he said, *"Tu mere saath baithega, yaa tere dost Pancham ke saath. Jaldi decide kar."* Fortunately, I had the presence of mind to tell Kaka-ji that I would chat with RDB for a while and join him later. That's because RDB was beckoning me to come towards him at the cocktail bar, as he wanted to share something with me. It was some grapevine gossip he had heard that same evening—RDB whispered and quizzed me whether 'it was true that a certain leading music composer-duo had professionally drifted apart, owing to some major personal differences.' When I told him 'it was quite true,' Pancham-da was shocked and visibly perturbed. Some other composer in his place would have treated it as *"khush khabri"*, as his rivals were going through a split-crisis. But at heart, RDB was a sensitive man who was also a well-wisher of his competitors. Incidentally, those days, there were no 'mobile phones,' so RDB put his whisky glass aside on the bar counter and said to me, 'Tomorrow morning I will try and speak to one of them, who is my buddy. I am sure their issues can be amicably resolved. This unpleasant development does not augur well for our showbiz industry.' He shrugged as he wore this genuine expression of concern.

Later, switching back to the merry party mood, he exchanged pleasantries and mingled with the cast of the movie, including heroine Dimple Kapadia, who was the co-hostess for the late-night party. Towards the fag end, Pancham was in his spirited mood as he hummed the refrain of his 'Aap Ki Kasam' song antaraa line 'Kuchh bhi ho lekin mazaa aa gaya meri jaan, hoye, O Kaka-ji, O Kaka-ji.' To which the Khanna, who plays a crusader journalist in the movie, in his trademark style, slanted his head and blinked. Even the celestial stars above must have skipped their heartbeat, I mean 'twinkle'!

Music release of 'QSQT'

Ek 'ladkay' ko dekha toh aisa lagaa

The music launch party of 'Qayamat Sey Qayamat Tak' was a historical milestone. Instead of the mandatory Searock, this was held at Hotel Centaur in its swanky Harbour Hall. This party had its significance, because out here 'guest of honour' R. D. Burman was metaphorically handing over his (legendary Nasir Hussain) 'banner baton' to the gen-next musical duo Anand-Milind and was specially invited to 'bless' the cast, including Aamir Khan and Juhi Chawla. In fact, I expected *khaas mehmaan* Pancham-da to turn up fashionably late. But I was in for a quirky surprise. As I marched ahead, a steward carrying a hoisted tray was holding a folded tissue paper on which was hastily scribbled *"peechay left side mein dekh."* Initially I wondered who it could be, and

I swerved around to find RDB waving out to me from a corner table behind a wide concrete column sitting. So I joined him for a brief chat, where he was profusely praising the musical calibre of Anand-Milind and Udit Narayan's singing. 'The songs are very impressive, and the album has the potential to strike it big,' enthused RDB, not displaying even an iota of jealousy or insecurity. As is common knowledge, they had gracefully 'replaced' him as decided by the young 'QSQT' director Mansoor Khan. The party was in full swing with every guest complimenting the 'QSQT' team. There was little boy Imran (who had played a cameo role of the young Aamir) who was cornering some of the attention. But one question that intrigued few of the guests was that the revered senior poet 'Majrooh-saab was retained' by the young Mansoor as the lyricist of 'QSQT.' When I asked RDB for his comments on not getting to compose for 'QSQT,' he nonchalantly replied, *"gaane gaane par likkha hai compose karne wale ka naam."* Charismatic hero **Aamir Khan, who considers Pancham-da among his few top favourites,** was on seventh heaven, even as the senior composer confidently predicted 'that the Khan would soon be the romantic sensation.'

At the 'Hare Rama Hare Krishna' star-studded premiere

Where Pancham-da was curious to know public reactions

No prizes for guessing that the vivacious Zeenat Aman (the media had fondly nicknamed her 'Zeenie baby') was the scene stealer at the star-studded premiere of debonair Dev Anand's **'Hare Rama Hare Krishna.'** The moment she arrived, there was a huge cheering uproar, and Dev Anand fondly received her. And then R. D. Burman walked in, and the massive crowd of star-gazers on the opposite road instantly recognized him and waved out to him. The late-night show was held at the plush newly opened Ganga theatre, which was part of the (now defunct) 'Ganga Jamuna' twin-theatres complex, which was a popular landmark in Tardeo at Mumbai Central. Already almost all the songs of 'Hare Rama ' composed by RDB had emerged chartbusters after the music had released, and 'Dum maro dum' was the hippie anthem, which had acquired a cult status. In those days, I was a secondary school student and I was already hooked on to the music of 'HRHK.' Since my residence was just a stone's throw away from the 'Ganga-Jamuna' theatres, I could manage to use my local contacts and get an invite pass to the premiere. When I entered the theatre foyer, I mustered up courage to go up to Dev-saab who was being mobbed and wish him. 'Thank you,' he said and nodded, I vividly remember, and then handed me a 'yellow rose' which he plucked from one of the stream of bouquets he had received at the theatre. Ironically, the 'musical hero' RDB was content standing away from the limelight with a couple of cine-industry buddies. That's when I grabbed the opportunity and went and handed him the same 'yellow rose' which Dev-saab had given me a few minutes ago. Pancham smiled as he patted me on my shoulder and asked me, "'Hare Rama' film *ka music sunaa? Kaisa lagaa?*"

I fumbled and said, 'Burman sir, it's too good, and all my classmates have loved it.' Then I requested him to sign his autograph on the reverse of the 'invitation pass,' as the cast and crew started moving into the theatre, occupying their allocated seats. As the movie screening concluded, I saw RDB briefly chatting with the non-filmy guests and asking them their 'frank feedback' on the two hippie-narcotics songs, which included the chorus of 'Hare Rama Hare Krishna.' Although Dev Anand had taken diligent precautions, yet there was an initial concern, whether the shock-value narcotics visuals songs could whip up a controversy. Interestingly, the movie had its entire rolling credits title music dedicated to chorus-chanting of the divine 'Hare Krishna' mantras. Of course, RDB's intoxicating music emerged the hottest chartbuster album of that year and until now the songs are 'smoking hot.' The Western songs 'Dum maro dum' and 'I love you' both catapulted Zeenat Aman overnight into a hallowed orbit. Her cavalier yet indelible image of the marijuana-smoking still reigns today (read Zeenat's ode to RDB in the Tributes section).

'Dil Padosi Hai' launch party on Asha Bhosle's B'day

Why RDB seemed uneasy at the fag end

In the showbiz industry, where 'media focus' is a must to survive and to thrive, RDB was an exception because he hardly hankered after publicizing himself. You will rarely come across RDB's birthday party celebration images during his lifetime. If at all, he used to celebrate privately with his core team musicians, close friends like producer Ramesh Behl, and star-hero Randhir Kapoor but he never used it as a pretext to grab press publicity. At the grand **'Dil Padosi Hai'** (1987) party held at the Hotel Taj Mahal Palace near the Gateway of India, the album release-day chosen was singing-diva Asha Bhosle's birthday (on 8 Sept). In sheer contrast to his Latino–American album 'Pantera,' released during the same year, 'DPH' was distinctly a non-filmy ad-lib, yet classy venture, which Pancham had dared to experiment. When I met RDB at this party, he was outwardly very exuberant, but I could sense something was amiss, which I will share later in this write-up.

Chief guest Sunil Dutt was in his elements as he spoke to me very casually. "*Pancham ki versatility ki daad deni padegi.* That man is a *sureela jadugar*! Out of thin air, he produces such brilliant variety of tunes. Actually I have heard only a few of the experimental yet sentimental songs of 'Dil Padosi Hai.' It was mainly because of the padosi-premika romantic numbers from 'Padosan' that RDB had became my favourite. When I approached RDB to help me launch my son Sunjay in 'Rocky' (1981), he assured me that he would create some immortal melodies. In fact in 'Rocky' we had 'three' lead screen characters for Sunju, Amjad-bhai, and Shakti Kapoor, all with the initials 'RD.' We were initially toying with the idea of making 'RDB' put in a cameo appearance as one of the judges. But since it was a dance competition situation, we then got Shammi Kapoor to play himself", Dutt-saab smiled as he mingled with the celeb guests. Later, the 'DPH' party progressed and 'prima donna' birthday girl Asha Bhosle was beaming with delight as she cut the customized heart-shaped chocolate birthday cake flanked by Gulzaar-saab and RDB, of course. Madame Asha gushed, saying, "*Yeh khubsoorat gaana* '*Bhenee bheene bhor,*' *hamare liye janamdin tohfa jaisa hi hai."* As I was leaving the party, I ambled towards Pancham-da to bid goodbye, and that's when Dada held my hand and took me to a corner of the banquet hall. 'There's some unpleasant unofficial whispers that I have been discreetly 'dropped' as the music composer for this movie being made by this big-banner leading director.' He looked distressed as he confided this 'volte face' development.

I was visibly perturbed. 'You mean there is no personal intimation?'

The sensitive RDB shook his head and said he would speak to me within a few days. 'But right now let this remain off the record,' he said with apprehension as he hugged me.

'Since this 'DPH' release has been such a joyous celebration, let's wait and hope for some positive development,' I responded, trying to console him as I took his leave.

Saagar movie premiere

'Yeh toh bataa tera feedback hai kya '

Departing from the conventional late-night-show norm, the star-studded premiere show of Ramesh Sippy's **'Saagar'** was an evening affair held at the renovated 'Excelsior' theatre in the vicinity of CST station in South Mumbai. The plush renovated theatre did not have the conventional separate upper balcony. By the time I reached, the 'houseful' show had already started. It was pitch dark, and I was standing near the balcony entrance, watching the movie with a group of people who had also come late. The music of 'Saagar' was classy with a range of classical and Western tracks, and I was keen to compliment Pancham-da. Hardly had I stood for ten minutes, when I felt a hand gently clawing me on my back. When I turned around, there were strangers behind. This happened again, but this time I stepped out from where I was standing and came a few steps ahead. Guess whom I saw? Not unexpected.

It was an impish Pancham-da standing outside behind the dark curtains and smoking. Looking a bit tense, he asked me whether the advance cine-trade reports of this movie were 'mixed.' Whatever I knew, I shared with him; I also told him that since the movie boasted of the comeback of the 'Bobby' hit screen couple Rishi and Dimple, the film ought to get a great opening. Besides, it also had the backing of his already popular RDB melodies. After hearing this, he seemed relieved. Extinguishing his just-lit 555 cigarette, he sneaked into the theatre and settled on his own seat in the VIP section in the rear rows. During the formal premiere ceremony on stage, there was a thundering applause for Pancham-da when his name was announced for him to come on stage with the star cast and main crew. Finally, the beaming audiences trickled out possibly with 'O yunhi gaate raho, ho muskurate raho' cavorting in their minds.

4

The Boss as seen through the eyes of his ace musicians

Panchamazing "Dream Team"
"All my songs have the signatures of my ace team of musicians and mera autograph" – Pancham
"Break the monotony—har baar kuchh toh alag karna hai" used to be his inspiring music mantra'

Honestly, I consider myself 'blessed' that R. D. Burman himself permitted me to attend the songs / background recordings / takes at Film Center. As far as possible, I tried to reach at least fifteen minutes before the rehearsals. And it was a cakewalk for me, as my residence was close to the recording studio. Even before Pancham-da would arrive, all the musicians would seem charged and enthusiastic, fine-tuning their instruments and checking the 'tone fitness.' The individual as well as the loyal collective dedication was **'panch-ama-zing.'** What I mean is that every musician felt the urge to add that extra 'zing' when he played his respective instrument. During one of the lunch breaks, I once asked RDB as what was the secret behind his getting the optimum outputs from his entire team while churning out a series of chartbusters. After a brief pause and a drag on his smoky cigarette, RDB revealed, **'My team does not work 'for' me. Rather they work 'with' me. All my songs have the signatures of my ace team of musicians and mera autograph.'**

"*Kya baat hai, Dada!* Well said!" I responded.

When I gently prodded him to elaborate, RDB came up with a **brilliant analogy.** "Once when I was travelling on Janmashtami Day in Bombay (now Mumbai), I was caught in a traffic jam and saw this six-tier human '*Govinda*' pyramid trying to access to the *dahi handi* (pot). What I keenly observed is that a massive crowd below was gazing at and gleefully cheering for 'only one man'—the only agile man who had clambered on to the top and was stretching his hands to clasp the rope and break the *handi.* That man had reached the top only because of the concerted 'shoulder support' given to him by the 'five tiers' of sturdy boys below. Similarly, only I get the limelight credit in the film titles and people applaud me for the music. But due credit also goes to the 'shoulder support' of my team of competent creative arrangers and finest musicians and, of course, the excellent sound recordists," he explained to me.

In the massive recording concert hall, the teams would generally be divided into the major sections—the strings section (group of violinists, guitars, cello etc), the brass section (saxophone, trombone, trumpet, clarinet etc), the rhythm section (tabla, dholak, drums, etc), the side percussions (duggi, maadal, chanda, tambourine, resso-resso, maracas etc). 'But there would always be a solidarity of harmony,' as RDB's music conductor-arranger late **Baablu-da Chakraborty** would point out.

Veteran vibraphone-player and rhythm-master **Burjor 'Buji' Lord** who played the drums for 'Dum maro dum' and 'I love you' reminisces, 'Sometimes I would spend sleepless nights anxiously wondering as to what RDB would ask me to play at the 'take' the next morning. Quite often we were told to deviate from the conventional. Like RDB would ask me to play on the rim of the drums or reverse the sticks and play or produce some weird scary sound on the crash cymbals. All the same, we were in awe of his quirky spontaneity', he chuckles.

Ace guitarist and virtuoso harmonica player **Bhanu-da Gupta** (who played the background 'mouth-organ' pieces for 'Sholay' as also the portions in the 'Yeh dosti' number, for instance) has tears welling in his eyes when he recalls how unassuming Pancham-da always gave him 'due credit' for any creative inputs or suggestions. 'Tell me how many other composers would shrug off the accolades from a legendary singer like Lata didi and tell her without any ego-issues, that I (Bhanu) was instrumental in fine-tuning the refrain of the dulcet song 'Kya yehi pyar hai.' And then Lata turns to me and showers her *taareef* on me. It was a memorable red-letter day for me. There is yet another *khushi ka kissa* where 'showman' film-maker Nasir Hussain presented Bhanu-da an imported Scotch whisky box. The prize-booze was for the *dhun* he suggested to Pancham-da for the title-song of 'Yaadon Ki Baaraat?' "*Bilkul sahi.* In fact, I have still carefully 'preserved' that same empty bottle of whisky which was more than a prestigious award for me," confides Gupta who has worked under the baton of several other 'rival' composers as well. "*But 'Boss' (RDB) ke saath mein kaam karne ka mazaa kuch anokha (unique) hi thaa.*" He shrugs with aplomb.

Eminent guitarist **Ramesh Iyer's** eyes light up with ecstasy yet tinged with sadness. 'There can never be another R. D. Burman, he was the aakhri musical maseeha who elevated film-music to its creative zenith. Pancham-da had an uncanny alert 'seventh sense' to spot anything that sounded different. For him every other mundane thing could produce harmonious sound (a glass, a bottle of water, a bunch of keys, a cup-saucer crashing) and even the human body was capable of making unconventional sounds (throat-gargle, wild screams and shrieks, backslapping, fillip (*chutki*) etc.) which could be blended into a song or background music. Even as we were 'strumming' during rehearsals, he would come and quietly stand behind and wait for us to play something off-beat ('don't use the plectrum,' try a metal tube) that would give him a 'brain-wave' and make us play those same notes, during the take. "*Break the monotony—har baar kucch toh alag karna hai*" used to be his inspiring music mantra,' asserts Iyer as he gazes at a portrait of his bohemian boss clad in his favourite red outfit. Almost every music session of our highly innovative boss was like a 'picnic-cum-surprise test.' We never knew what would be in store. 'Expect the unexpected was his tag-line that defined him,' avers Iyer, who has played classy guitar pieces in the original soundtracks of hundreds of hit songs including the ones in 'Saagar.'

Eminent accordion, keyboards and rhythm player and an acclaimed wizard of weird sound effects and 'echo-delay' effects **Kersi Lord,** who was with Pancham right from 'day one' feels that his otherwise exuberant Boss was a 'hard taskmaster' who would never take 'no' for an answer. Recalls **Lord,** 'Whenever he wanted any kind of bizarre simulated sound effect or echo effects, he would ask me to get it 'organized.' There was no way I could 'back out.' It had to be executed by hook or by crook. Even if I showed signs of a skeptical response, RDB would storm me with 'why have I kept you—I know you can do it.' But I realized that with these utterly crazy yet creative challenges he brought out the best in me' laughs **Kersi,** who is also popular for his instant zany humour like RDB.

Virtuoso violinist and award-winning composer **Uttam Singh** who has played most of the solo violin pieces for RDB's songs (like for instance in the interlude of the award-winning 'Kya hua tera vaada') flows into a recall mode. Reveals **Uttam,** 'Genius RDB who could easily compose two to three quality songs a day. Like Shahenshah Akbar, Dada had the whole-hearted creative support from his *'navratna'* (nine gems) core team of musicians at his 'sittings.' That's where the song would be born and honed to perfection. At the actual recordings, we would wait eagerly for boss to exclaim 'KBH,' which is the short-form of *'Kya Baat Hai'* and our day would be made. If a musician or a singer made minor errors, he would generally say 'KBN' which stands for *'Koi Baat Nahin.'* There was some in-born superhuman talent that RDB was blessed with—you know, he could easily compose two to three terrific songs in a day. Whereas composers like me would probably take sometimes a week or even more, to independently compose and finalise just two outstanding songs (laughs). Rarely have I seen RDB losing his temper and getting nasty. But yes, it has happened, and he would cool down later. But at heart he was a jolly-good-fellow. We will always miss him,' says Singh wistfully.

Late master percussionist **Homi-da Mullan,** who was part of the core team, exclaimed that 'every take of RDB was like an informal *imtihaan* of our creative inputs, but we enjoyed it. Because the verbal 'result-report card' was given to us before 'pack-up' on the same day, by the Chancellor of music, by way of his sheer approval.' Continued **Homi-da**, 'Whenever I was invited to play at various 'live' RDB memorial concerts, playing his compositions was like a 'rejuvenating tonic.' And I am so grateful to the passionate **Team Panchammagic (Pune)** for actively involving me at their bi-annual seminars on RDB. That again is so mentally stimulating and I could feel the 'soulful' presence of boss at all their events.' **Mullan** smiled**.**

Acclaimed singer and excellent guitarist **Bhupinder Singh** (who also plays the 12-strings guitar) opines that 'despite any pre-set musical themes or notations, the ad-lib scope to improvise, innovate was with affable Pancham-da.' Recalls Bhupi-da, "I once lost a bet of Rs. 100/- in 1973 with RDB when I could not figure out -which English tune he had been inspired by. Strangely, both of us went 'together' to watch that English movie 'If Its Tuesday This Must Be Belgium' at the New Empire theatre. The basic English tune was adapted only in the initial refrain of 'Chura liya hai,'" chuckles Singh.

Noted classical flautist **Ronu Majumdar** who segued into RDB's filmy team playing flute notes for RDB's chartbusting songs in the 80's, seems overwhelmed as he enthuses, "Actually I owe my musical personality development mainly to Pancham-da. During the recording of 'Kucch Na Kaho,' Dada allowed me the creative freedom to play the '*baansuri*' using 'dragging notes'. You can still experience the surreal resonating results."

Outstanding maadal-player **Ranjit 'Kaancha' Gazmer** and adroit resso-resso player **Amrutrao Katkar** both recall how RDB would treat all musicians as his 'equals.' 'Whenever we were having food from our tiffins during the lunch-break, Dada would pick up large chunks and morsels from our '*dabbas*,' especially if it was very pungent *(tikkha)*. Conversely, if he brought non-vegetarian khaana, which he had himself 'cooked' he would joyfully share it with us,' they reveal.

For rhythm-maestro **Franco Vaz** who played the drums from 'Kasme Vaade' onwards upto 'Gardish,' 'my 'boss' RDB had rhythm flowing in his blood and his genes.' Elaborates **Franco**, 'What was commendable is that Dada would give me creative freedom to play the beats that I felt was right. Sometimes when he felt that my rhythm pattern was not suited to that specific song, he would coax me to play some other innovative beats. Twenty weeks later, he would come and remind me, 'Franco, remember five months ago you played that rhythm beat which I had not okayed. I want you to play that same pattern of beats again for this new song today. Gosh what a memory, man. *Maan gaye Rahul-da,*' gushes **Franco** who had played the impressive solo roll on roto-toms and tympani in the mukhdaa of the title song 'Rocky mera naam.'

Tailpiece: The final sentimental 'last words' come from the saxophone supremo, late Manohari-da Singh also a whistling wizard who also played the mandoline. 'Perfection, excellence and dynamic variety marked all his recordings. My association with Pancham has been so enriching and emotional that I fervently pray to God, that even in my agley janam, I should 'once again' be assisting our beloved 'Boss' Rahul-da' smiled Manohari-da when I had met him diligently rehearsing on the saxophone for the 'Gulabi aankhen' song, much before the curtains swirled open, at an RDB concert at the ISKCON auditorium. 'Although I know my pieces very well, yet I can't take any chance. Because 'Boss' is watching from above,' he said softly. It left me speechless. Yet another realization of what it 'meant' to be part of the RDB's dream-team.

Fish, football, fusion and check-mating in chess were among RDB's favorites. Recounts senior film-publicist Ajit Ghosh, one of Pancham-da's close associates for over two decades, 'When it came to relishing fresh fish, he would sometimes personally go out of his way with me, to fetch them from distant markets. As far as his ailing health was concerned, he had a very casual approach. Although he had a high level of diabetes and was advised against excess drinking because of his cardiac conditions, he seemed a bit flippant about it. Never was he keen to hype himself in the media, preferring to let fate take its own course. A rebel by nature, he lived life on his own terms. For me, the lovable buddy Panchamda is still around—since his music is immortal.'

5

Burman-da's Brazilian (football & music) connection

The innovative genius Pancham-da was an ardent football freak. While his favourite *desi* team was East Bengal, he would make occasionally make it a point to sneak out to the Mumbai city Cooperage grounds with his buddies to watch football matches.

After returning from watching the deft dribbling and agile goal-scoring sessions, RDB would, at times, rush to the Film Center recording studio and get his assistants to write fresh improvised music notations. 'Watching football at home on TV or in the stadium, actually gives me an inspirational 'kick.' In music you write the 'score' and in soccer it's the goal-score' was his favourite repartee.

The rhythm-savvy RDB had a fetish for anything that had a Brazilian tag. Their pulsating music, their vibrant dances, their musical instruments especially the tug-friction drum 'cuica' which he had specially bought **when he visited Rio De Janeiro** during their spectacular 'carnival.' This 'cuica' instrument, which produces a weird sound like a puppy-dog yelping, was played by ace drummer Franco Vaz in the hit RDB Bengali song 'Macher Kaanta.' Their famous football team, with their legendary 'forward' player **Pele** was his all-time favourite. Among RDB's favorite Brazilian rhythms was the **'bossa nova,'** and he blended those foot-tapping beats in a large number of his chartbuster numbers. An ideal instance of R D Burman being inspired by a racy Brazilian tune which goes Verão Vermelho (by Brazilian singer Elis Regina) is evident in this vibrant song 'Jeevan ke har mod pe' (Jhootha Kahin Ka, 1979).

Call it a brain drain of sorts, but Pancham-da's Latin–American album Pantera (1987), released in South America, had caught the fancy of the Brazilian youth.

Among RDB's prime regrets was that cricket-obsessed India never qualified for the FIFA World Cup.

An uncanny coincidence for die-hard Pancham fans who are also hooked on to soccer, is that the year (1994) in which he passed away, Brazil won the FIFA World Cup. And in 2014, when it was RDB's platinum (75th) birth anniversary, the venue was Brazil!!!!!

✿✿Viver para sempre musica rei senhor Pancham-da!

✿✿ Live forever music king, Lord Pancham-da (Brazilian national language-Portugese)

6

'With its 'soul' rhythm beat and 'wah-wah' to start with, cult hippie anthem 'Dum maro dum' had to be immortal': Pancham-da (RDB)

Way back in 1971, when he casually composed it, music virtuoso Rahul Dev Burman must have hardly anticipated that his evergreen infectious disco-hippie anthem 'Dum maro dum' would have umpteen remixes and would eventually be voted 'the song of the millennium' by a legion of FM 'radio-active' listeners. Not just that, four decades later, an entire film would be titled 'Dum maro dum' produced by 'showman' Ramesh Sippy. **In one of his masti-mazaak moods, the legendary singer Kishore Kumar had once quipped, that the 'DMD' track was powerful enough to make a 'dead' person come 'alive'!** In the course of my frequent personal interview-interactions with RDB, at Film Center recording studios, the modest composer once briefly shared with me the 'making of 'Dum maro dum.' Revealed Rahul-da, 'The lyrics of the *mukhda* were written quite casually by Bakshi-saab based on local lingo used by young streetside boys who loved to smoke. Once that was done I did not have to make much of an effort to set the lyrics to the tune.

In the song, my special RDB touch was the stretched 'dummmaaaah' and the 'gummmaaaah,' in the mukhdaa, to suggest the 'inhaling' and 'exhaling' and the nashaa generated. It was a challenge for me to create the frenzied *mahaoul* of the marijuana-den, which Dev-saab had briefed me. Honestly, the credit also goes to my superb musicians.

For the first time, I think, in Hindi film music, we used the 'soul rhythm' beat, which was played on the drums by Burjor ('Buji') Lord. Since the song has its 'soul,' I guess it had to be immortal (laughs). Secondly, eminent singer-guitarist Bhupinder Singh, while strumming for producing the riff, also used an imported 'wah-wah' pedal attached to the electric guitar, to produce the haunting intro overture. There was the chorus chanting, while Charanjit Singh played the transichord for the 'drone' effect, to generate the perfect intoxicating mood for the song. So indirectly we also got our 'wah-wah,' even as the song was being recorded.' RDB chuckled.

Recalls jovial ace drummer 'Burjor,' while rapping the drums for this song, I could imagine the vivacious Zeenat Aman swaying to my pulsating beats. But then I had this 'hunch' that this 'dum-daar' song would emerge a trendsetter,' shrugs 'Buji.'

Wasn't it true, that film-maker-actor Dev Anand initially 'rejected' 'Dum maro dum,' as he felt that it would 'totally eclipse' his follow-next sermonising song 'Dekho o deewano' in the same movie? RDB was initially reticent on this touchy issue. But after a bit of prodding he had opened up with the condition that he would prefer to speak 'off-the-record' at that point of time. 'Quite true. It was a tough time for us to collectively convince Dev-saab to include 'Dum maro dum' in the movie. In fact, he reluctantly agreed to use only *"one mukhda-one antaraa"* of that song in the movie, that too after a lot of coaxing and cajoling,' revealed RDB.

Actually Usha Iyer-Uthup with her husky voice discloses that she was being considered originally for this 'DMD' song. But as destiny decided, it was recorded by melody-queen Asha Bhosle, and it became an all-time iconic song. Nevertheless, Usha sang the fabulous English-Hindi number 'I Love You' along with madame Bhosle for 'Hare Rama'

Two decades later, when **I personally met Dev-saab** at his 'Anand' penthouse on his birthday (26 Sept.), I dared to broach this sensitive issue of him marginalizing the 'DMD' cult song and he offered his version. 'It was the first time I was working with Pancham independently, so I had to get attuned to his different style of Western music. The movie 'HRHK' begins with the authentic chorus chanting of Hare Krishna mantras by his genuine devotees and there is a strong social message in my next song 'Dekho o deewano.' Which is why, it was my moral responsibility to also ensure that 'drug-abuse' should not get glorified,' justified Dev-saab.

Curiously, RDB also experimented by recording a 'remix' of his own 'Dum maro dum' with a different Latin American fast-paced rhythm in the medley that follows the song 'Dill mill gaye' ('Yaadon Ki Baarat') way back in 1973. But, somehow, fans did not get hooked onto this funky track although it was picturised on the same 'DMD' glam-diva Zeenie baby. Apparent reason: there was no 'soul rhythm beat' this time in the 'remixed' version. It was also featured in the 2003 Bollywood movie 'Boom' where Zeenat Aman once sways and swings to the 'DMD' track. But it proved futile, as the multi-starrer bohemian film vanished like smoke from a toke.

As the celebrated songstress **Asha Bhosle** who won the Filmfare Best Female Playback Award for her 'DMD' song stormed, 'If someone constructs a replica Taj Mahal mini-monument elsewhere in India, will people stop going to Agra? Remixes may come and disappear, but the original 'DMD' reigns on forever,' she smiles, raising her right fist symbolically.

Interestingly the infectious 'soul' rhythm beat with 'minor variations' have been used in numerous chartbuster RDB songs. Some instances of the 'soul-beat' RDB numbers:

1. Aap ke kamre mein koi rehta hai (Yaadon Ki Baarat)
2. Jaane-jaan dhoondta (Jawani Diwani)

3. Saare ke saare gama (Parichay)

4. Yeh jawani hai diwani (Jawani Diwani)

5. Omaaji omaaji re (Bandhe Haath)

6. Shubhu shubu refrain in aaj ki raat koi (Anamika)

7. Dil mein jo mere samaa gayi (Jhoota Kahin Ka)

Tailpiece: In an original innovative deviation, musicians played the Western 'soul' beats on the ethnic 'tabla,' for this song 'Bhor bhaye panghat pe.' It's from 'showman' Raj Kapoor's 'Satyam Shivam Sundaram' (1978) which has its Filmfare Award-winning music scored by Laxmikant Pyarelal, who shared a warm 'personal' rapport with Pancham-da. And this 'soul' rhythm song was yet again picturised on village belle Zeenat Aman 'catwalking' thru lush greenery and cascading water.

Tail-Twist: A testimony to Pancham-da's innovative streak is the way he has given a total 'soul' rhythmic 'make-over' to this song 'Aap ke kamre mein' (1973). The song has its inspirations apparently derived from the rolling title-music of 'Sujata' (1959) which had S. D. Burman's music, where son Rahul was an assistant. And a decade later from this Bengali song 'Bondho darer ondhokaare' from 'Rajkumari' (1970) which, of course, had RDB's music.

7

By Invitation—Guest Article

Yeh kya hua, kaise hua, kab hua, kyun hua

Eminent Bollywood Film Director ANANTH MAHADEVAN unravels the challenge of making a highly 'difficult' tribute film to R. D. Burman, that too with the title of a chartbuster Laxmi-Pyare hit song, that is, 'Dil Vil Pyar Vyar.'

"When India's seminal composer Rahul Dev Burman departed prematurely in 1994 at the age of fifty-four, there wasn't the faintest indication that his work would flag off my journey as a film-maker. What was to transpire at the turn of the millennium would write a new chapter in Indian cinema. The use of published music in a different context, that not only paid tribute to the original works, but underlined the void created by the composer who has yet to find a worthy successor, though A. R. Rahman's notes hark back to the path breaking beginning of Pancham- da.

"It was the spring of 2001. Producer Viveck Vaswani and I were ensconced in his office, discussing the possibility of 'three love stories' intermingling with select R. D. Burman's numbers. It was a task cut out for me. And as a debut film, it was asking for trouble. Which songs from the 330 odd films that he composed for would make the cut. Would it resemble the popular film songs show on TV *Chhaya Geet* where songs were merely strung together? And to add to our challenge, we had titled the film 'Dil Vil Pyar Vyar,' incidentally a Laxmikant Pyarelal chartbuster from the film 'Shagird,' which ruled out the possibility of a title track.

'Dil Vil Pyar Vyar' had three tales boy meets girl [Jimmy Shergill-Hrishita Bhatt], boy loses girl [R. Madhavan-Namrata Shirodkar] and boy regains girl [Sanjay Suri-Sonali Kulkarni]. It offered an exciting possibility of delving into every genre of music that Pancham-da had attempted. Even the colours in the love stories depicted the moods of the characters. And so the exercise began. The film had scope for 14 numbers, but the million dollar question was, 'Which ones?????'

"The immediate next step was to procure the recording rights to the iconic composer's works. Since HMV had the lion's share of his albums in their repertory, Vaswani and me decided to approach Harish Dayani, then CEO of the company. The concept of reworking the maestro's numbers sounded innovative to Dayani who made it a win-win situation. HMV would part with the rights of the songs without charging a fee and in return would hold the rights to the new soundtrack of 'Dil Vil Pyar Vyar.' The selection of the numbers to feature in the film was left entirely to our discretion. Of course, rumours floated around of the original producers like Nasir Husain being displeased with the deal that HMV had made, as they did not stand to benefit from their own creations.

"The selection was a tricky exercise. Songs had to be picked to match a situation. And the rugged 'rider' was that the lyrics had to justify the occasion too, as the words could not be tampered with. So when Jimmy Shergill had to give chase to Hrishita Bhatt on a local train, 'Oh haseena zulfonwali' fitted in perfectly. We even tweaked one of the lines and incorporated the titular 'Dil Vil Pyar Vyar' phrase in this 'Teesri Manzil' number. When the three boys came together after being disillusioned in love and drunk the night out, 'Yeh Jo Mohabbat Hai' seemed tailor-made for the situation. It was indeed uncanny, how each of the 14 numbers appeared to be written for scenes from the film. It was a tough call to drop my all time favourite 'Rim jhim gire sawan' to accommodate 'Ab ke sawan mein jee jale' which was more appropriate to the sequence with Suri and Kulkarni. And a pity that

By Invitation—Guest Article

numbers from 'Jawani Diwani' like 'Jaane jaan' couldn't be considered as the publishing company was Polydor.

"When the news spread that a film based on Pancham-da compositions was under production, music directors who had sought inspiration from the late composer, sent in feelers to work on the recreation of the soundtrack. But most of them ended up in conjugating the originals with 'modern touches' that made them sound like 'remixes.' Vaswani and I had one common agenda. The arrangements could be upgraded, but the songs would remain a tribute, not a victim of the fad of remixes. That was where Babloo Chakraborty stepped in.

He was Pancham-da's faithful associate and arranger for decades and qualified to retain the soul of his compositions while rearranging the same for a new generation. His improvisations were so masterly, that the late maestro would have been pleased. Babloo Chakraborty faithfully placed a portrait of his mentor Dada on the recording console each day and sought his blessings before commencing a day's work. His allegiance was highly touching.

"New age singers like Abhijeet Bhattacharya, Babul Supriyo, ghazal maestro and pop-singer Hariharan and Shanker Mahadevan were in for a surprise as they were called on to negotiate the genius of Pancham's notes. Kavita Krishnamurthy, who came in to record, what she thought was a regular day in office, was taken aback that she had to reprise the Lata Mangeshkar golden oldie 'Kya janoo sajan hoti hai kya gham ki shaam.' Initially, she shied away from attempting to sing it, when her husband, the violin maestro Dr. L. Subramaniam, stepped in. 'There's no harm in giving it your interpretation. A song is, after all, a song.' That spurred her on and her rendition of the number had a haunting quality of its own. Recently when Dr. L. Subramaniam composed the score for one of my biopics Gour Hari Dastaan—the freedom file, Kavita and I had a hearty laugh recalling her reservations. She now remembers the song very fondly.

"The album, a double compact disc release, did for HMV what their releases over the past decade could not achieve. Their balance sheets brightened up again and 'Dil Vil Pyar Vyar' was a bestseller that they included in their catalogue. Of course, the critics and detractors were quite a few. While rumour had it that Asha Bhosle was displeased with the idea of her husband's work being tampered with, Narendra Kusnur a music critic openly criticized the concept at our trailer launch. The words hurt, since we had meant it to be a tribute and not to cash in on the popularity of the composer's hits. But redemption came the following week when the film opened in cinemas. Kusnur was so enamoured by the way the songs were integrated into the script, that he was honest enough to take his words back in a published review in the tabloid Mid Day. In fact the paper published two reviews, one that of its regular critic and the other, Kusnur's. In fact, he admitted to 'enjoy the film a lot.' We stood vindicated.

"Dil Vil Pyar Vyar was my 'baptism by fire.' I had wanted to make a directorial debut film that would be entertaining as well as memorable. Pancham-da's music and the late Sujit Sen's script helped me achieve both. It became India's first-ever 'retro musical.' It made many scratch their heads and say aloud 'why the hell didn't we think of it before.' The film today is telecast at least once a week on prime time movie channels. It has been deemed, a cult film. That describes Pancham-da's work too absolutely cult. Which composer would have dreamt up the evocative, operatic 'Jaago sone walo' in Bhoot Bungla during those days? I was the lucky one who got away with it. My debut film's poster said MUSIC: R. D. BURMAN. Incidentally, we had planned to name the three boys in the film as Rahul, Dev and Burman. But then it sounded too obvious. The legend would have been flattered though.'

– **Ananth Mahadevan**

8

Indelible Stamp of Genius

< Why Five >

A rare special commemorative Rs. 5/- Postage Stamp image featuring two pictures of the *mahaan* genius *sangeetkar* (music composer) is a philatelic souvenir with his loyal die-hard fans. The 'Rs.5/-' value matches Pancham's mascot number 5 as he considered number 5 lucky. As is known, Pancham means the 'Fifth Musical Note' and even his favourite Fiat car registration number was 1139 which adds up to 1+ 4 = '05.' The turning point mega-hit movie 'Teesri Manzil' was the 'fifth' movie in his career. The icing on the cake is that his name Rahul also has 'five' letters. Most of the time, he would carry with him his favourite pack of State Express '555' brand of cigarettes.

One of the color pictures on the stamp clicked by the author Chaitanya Padukone, has Pancham-*da* striking a 'pose' on the synthesizers. Otherwise an ardent RDB fan, Chaitanya had the privileged opportunity to attend dozens of Pancham-da's song recordings, while taking his interviews at Film Center (Tardeo, in South Mumbai). The various candid interviews of RDB taken by Padukone were published in a Mumbai city tabloid newspaper in the '80s and the '90s.

Recalls the author Chaitanya, 'Way back in July 1983, I asked Pancham-*da* to pose on the tympani drums-set and also on the keyboards at Film Center (Tardeo) during the background score of the film 'Mazdoor.' But the media-shy Pancham-da was initially reluctant, as normally he did not play the keyboards at sittings, but preferred the desi harmonium. *"Mujhe thodi acting karni padegi,"* he chuckled and also insisted then, that I should 'not' publish those photos along with his print-media interviews.

Then he posed again for the author's camera, sitting at the digital recording mixer-console, which was eventually published with the newspaper-interviews. Now that the melody-wizard has left his indelible 'stamp' on the retro-music map of Bollywood, the postal stamp is indeed a token tribute to his musical legacy.

9

Pancham-da's zany sense of Humour

'Woh 'chuppa rustom' niklaa **and RDB proved that he was a better comedian than me'** —Mehmood-Bhaijaan

Besides his innate aptitude for composing tunes instantly, (like the way cash cascades from an 'ATM,' here the 'M' stands for 'melody') Pancham-da had this penchant for humorous punch-lines and playing pranks. Before and after the recordings, and at parties he was usually in his witty elements. Once when I met him at a showbiz party 'Dada' asked me in a serious tone, as to which course I had done to qualify as a film-journalist, so I shared with him the details, the amount of fees etc. That's when RDB responded with: **'Why did you waste your hard-earned money. All you need to do, is to 'hum' my composed song**—*'Yeh kya hua, kaise hua, kab hua, kyun hua'* **and isn't that the essence of journalism.** Am I right?' And I burst out laughing. In this book, you will come across various other instances of RDB's *hansi-mazaak* wala nature.

Former popular actress and **Kishore Kumar's wife Leena Chandavarkar-Ganguly** vividly recalls how RDB would record and send songs like his own 'Pallo latke' with **naughty-masti lyrics** and ask his *jigri dost* Kishore-da to hear it discreetly with head-phones. 'When I used to hear KK laughing out loudly, all by himself, I used to wonder what was he fantasizing. Then I realized the *"andar ki baat"*,' reveals Leena who also remembers how RDB used to make her chuckle with his witticisms. '**Thank God, laughter is tax-free,**' the composer would also say. Recalls team RDB ace veteran musician **Kersi Lord,** '**Whenever he would make people laugh, Rahul-da would derive pleasure out of it**. Often, from behind, he would swoop on to the 'ticklish' musicians and suddenly tickle them from behind. Like jack-in-the box, they would spring up in the air. Even the canteen tea-boy was not spared by Pancham,' smiles Lord. Since RDB was fond of red outfits, **Gulzar used to fondly call him** *"lal kauwa"* (red crow). Not one to take things lying down **Pancham reciprocated** by referring to **Gulzar as** *"safed kauwa"* (**white crow**) as the illustrious lyricist-director always wore starched white ethnic libaas. Recalls TV serial director **Tarun Mathur, "We realized** RDB also has a funny bone for loud laughing, that too in sync with the melody. Besides humming the title-lyrics backed by the chorus-singers and music pieces, **Pancham-da recorded crazy variations of guffawing laughter in his 'own voice'** for the title music of his buddy Rajesh Khanna's TV serial 'Aadha Sach Aadha Jhooth.'"

Producer Barkha Roy ('Sanam Teri Kasam') fondly remembers how RDB had this rare ability to laugh at himself. After he returned from his 'by-pass' surgery from London, Pancham jestfully said to me, *"Yeh by-pass ke baad, lagta hai mere producers jo paas thhe, kaafi door ho gaye.* Before they bypass me, I have to surpass the odds. Now that cardiac surgeon Dr. Mukesh Hariawala has given me a new lease of life and a rejuvenated heart, I will get the *'tez dhadkan'* back in my music. All of us have rhythm in our bodies, that's why the heart and the pulse have their 'beats.'"

During his lifetime, legendary comedy-badshah **Mehmood-bhaijaan** who was RDB's mentor, once accidentally met me at a late-night party. After speaking generally about happenings in showbiz, the topic changed to Burman Junior. There was a blushing glow on **Mehmood's** face as he said, *'Pataa hai* Pancham is an excellent comedian off-screen. That's how I got him to play a cameo in 'Bhoot

Bungla.' Almost all the funny facial expressions shots which he gave were improvised by him. *Woh 'chuppa rustom' niklaa* **and RDB proved that he was better than me.** We had actually tricked him into giving the first shot by drenching him and then 'continuity'*ka bahaana banaake*, we made him face the camera for many more scenes. There were the trick photography-editing shots where our necks were shown 'rotating' 360 degrees—even our necks were also into *"aao twist karen"* mood. **In fact, I wanted him to play Bhola's character in 'Padosan' but he was reluctant.** And then the box-office pressures made us opt for a regular lead actor Sunil Dutt. Since Nasir Hussain-saab managed to cast him in 'Pyar Ka Mausam' (1969), we were contemplating that he play'himself' along with Kishore Kumar in the laugh-riot 'Bombay to Goa'(1972). But *ek baar phir*, he declined, but Kishore-da agreed,' said Mehmood and chuckled, whose hilarious song **'Todi naakh tabla, ne phodi naakh petti'** ('Vardaan') sung by him in a weird croaky voice under the baton of Kalyanji-Anandji would highly amuse RDB, and he loved listening to that track.'

Twist-in-the-Tale: '*Late' film-maker Arun Dutt directed this romantic movie 'Khule Aam'(1992) under his legendary father 'Guru Dutt Films' banner. This film had its music scored by RDB. Apparently, the film was screened for foreign delegates abroad, where they sub-titled the movie in English as 'Open Mangoes.' Once the 'gaffe' was pointed out, they made the correction. On hearing this, the witty Panchamda said to Arun, "What if the title was 'Aam Aadmi' — would they refer to it as the 'Mango-Man'?" This anecdote was shared with me by Arun himself in December 2007 when we partied together.*

Once, I happened to casually ask 'Tublu,' RDB that is, during the 80s at a film party as to why he 'used to' fondly carry his 'mouth-organ' with him most of the time. With his flair for witty repartees, he had quipped 'How could I forget it? It's har-monica, O my darling!'

PART 2

PanchaMontage

Rare, startling posed and candid RDB Images
Jidhar dekhun, teri tasveer, nazar aati hai.

Courtesy: Viju Katkar

Playful RDB with his
musician, Viju Katkar.

Courtesy : B K Tambe

Gulzar chats with Asha Bhosle at
Marylands apartment.

Rajesh Khanna being interviewed by the author.

Courtesy: Leena Chandavarkar - Ganguly

RDB with his manager Bharat Ashar
(centre), Amit Kumar and Shailendra Singh.

Courtesy: Leena Chandavarkar-Ganguly.

RDB with Leena, Sumeet and their
dog Benny.

RDB at Film Center—Melody
mein twist.

Rhythm king RDB poses against the
Tympani drums, metallic maadal
and the grand piano at Film Center.

RDB with Shabbir Kumar, Lata Mangeshkar, Dharmendra, Sunny and Amrita
at the 'Betaab' song recording.

Annual meeting of all leading Bollywood
composers—RDB is in the front row—third from left.

RDB with Leena Chandavarkar
Ganguly.

Courtesy: Jatin Wagle

RDB with Amitabh Bachchan, Rajesh Khanna and producer Satish Wagle at 'Namak Haraam.' song recording.

Vidhu Vinod Chopra with Jackie Shroff.

Courtesy: Chin2 Bhosle

Asha Bhosle with grandson singer Chin2 Bhosle.

Courtesy: Shyam & Jagdish Aurangabadkar

Dev Anand and RDB watch as Asha Bhosle and Kishore-da rehearse their lines.

Courtesy: Poornima

RDB, Raj Kapoor, Randhir Kapoor, Sachin-da and Poornima (Sushma Shrestha) at 'Ek din bik jaayega' song recording of 'Dharam Karam.'

Courtesy: Amit Kumar

Unveiling of RDB statue on Jan 4th 2014,in Kolkata, initiated by the Amit Kumar Fans Club in the presence of Amit Kumar and Usha Uthup.

Courtesy: Leena Chandavarkar-Ganguly

RDB with Kishore, Asha and Lata.

Courtesy: Ashim Samanta

At RDB's wedding reception—father Sachin-da with guests Shakti-da and Mehmood.

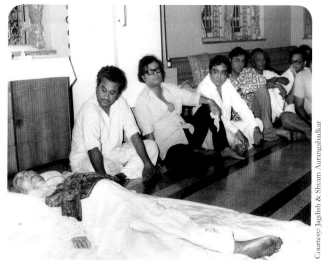

Courtesy: Jagdish & Shyam Aurangabadkar

'Woh phir nahin aate' ... Sad demise of his father Sachin Dev Burman–
Among those who came to condole Pancham were Kishore Kumar, Prakash
Mehra, Rajendra Kumar, Naushad, Gulzar & Asha Bhosle (not in pic).

Courtesy: Ashim Samanta

RDB, Shakti-da, Uttam Kumar
and Rajesh Khanna.

Courtesy: Ashim Samanta.

RDB with Shakti Samanta and Rajesh
Khanna–yeh shaam mastani.

Courtesy: Shyam & Jagdish Aurangabadkar

RDB with his rhythm section chief
Maruti Rao, Mohammed Rafi and
'buddy' Mehmood.

Courtesy: Anandji-bhai.

'Saviour' RDB performs at
Kalyanji–Anandji Nite.
(refer page 104)

Ramesh Behl, RDB and Asha Bhosle—
Agar saaz chheda taraane banenge.

RDB and Asha Bhosle as 'guests' at a
wedding reception.
Keh doon tumhe, yaa chup rahun.....

RDB's debonair suited look.

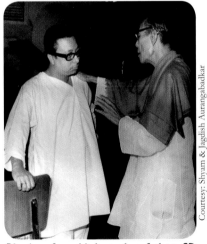

Blessings from his legendary father, SD
Burman—*Safal hogi teri aradhana.*

Panchamda with Asha and Lata—they
have sung peppy RDB 'duets' like 'Main
chali main chali' and 'Lavangi mirchi'

Courtesy: Shyam & Jagdish Aurangabadkar

Chief Guest RDB with Udit Narayan, Anand and Milind at the Qayamat Se Qayamat Tak music launch party.

RDB at RK movies launch with 'Showman' Raj Kapoor, with his star-sons Randhir, Rishi and Rajiv.

Blockbuster 'Sholay' movie release party in Bangalore—RDB, Amitabh Bachchan, Ramesh Sippy, GP Sippy and Amjad Khan.

RDB with Asha B at Lions' Club Awards event - 1986 (Note their dress colour co-ordination)

RDB with SDB and Lata–*hothon mein aisi baat, main dabaake chali aayi?*

Courtesy: Raj Sippy

Courtesy: Barkha Roy

RDB at song recording of 'Satte Pe Satta' with Bhupinder, director Raj Sippy, Gulshan Bawra, Asha and Kishore Kumar.

RDB with Asha Bhosle and producer Barkha Roy at the song recording of 'Sanam Teri Kasam,' which fetched RDB his first Filmfare Award.

Courtesy: Devi Dutt

Courtesy: Asha Bhosle.

RDB at the recording of the song 'Tujh se naaraz' for the film 'Masoom' with Devi Dutt, Gulzar, singer Anup Ghoshal, Javed Akhtar, Mahendra Jain and director Shekhar Kapur.

RDB with Basu, Manohari and Maruti—the core team.

Courtesy: Shyam & Jagdish Aurangabadkar

Young RDB with 'Masoom' producer Devi Dutt in 1964.

RDB, Manohari-da, and Anand Bakshi at Shakti Samanta's music 'sitting.'

Courtesy: Chaitanya P

Marylands, first floor—RDB's landmark apartment where scores of chartbuster songs were composed during music 'sittings.'

Ranjit Gazmer on the maadal (Nepali mini-drums) and Homi Mullan on duggi. RDB's mandatory signature sounds were played on these (percussion) instruments in almost every second song.

Courtesy: Pyarelal

RDB's favourite recording centre – Film Center Building, Tardeo.

RDB with Pyarelal– *Yeh dosti hum nahin todenge.*

Courtesy: Bhupinder Singh

Courtesy: Vimal Kumar

RDB on bongos, Bhupinder on tumba and Ranjit on maadal at the background recording of suspense music.

RDB with Kishore K, producer Vimal Kumar, Gulshan B and recordist Kaushik at the song recording of the award-winning title song 'Agar tum na hote'

Courtesy: Raj Sippy

RDB at the release of the album 'Andar Baahar' with N N Sippy, Raj Sippy, Jackie Shroff and Ashok Mehta.

Courtesy: Ranjit Gazmer

RDB and Gogi lunch at Kaancha's house – notice how impulsive Pancham-da is helping himself with the portions of food.

Courtesy: Tariq

Rockstar Tariq Khan. *Tum kya jaano 'stardom' kya hai.*

Courtesy: Anand-ji

RDB with Laxmikant, Anandji and Pyarelal—note the harmonica in RDB's left hand and their mutual harmony despite the competition.

RDB's autograph

भारत
INDIA
2007
S. D. BURMAN
15.00

S.D. Burman postage stamp

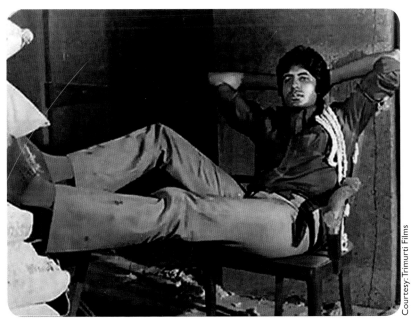

Courtesy: Trimurti Films

No songs for Big B—but brillant background music in 'Deewar'.

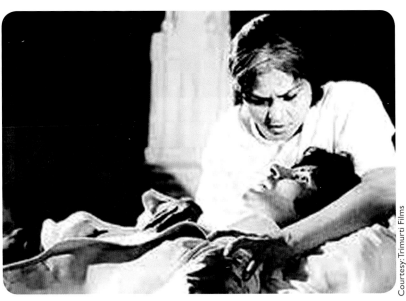

Courtesy: Trimurti Films

'Deewaar' climax scene—Amitabh Bachchan and Nirupa Roy.

To score a hit you need to add your punch

High-pitched R D Burman

Courtesy: Chaitanya P

RDB being interviewed by the author at Film Center (July 1983).

Note how Pancham-da seems so relaxed with both his feet folded on the sofa, minus the shoes, as he is animatedly conversing with the author. An unlit cigarette is dangling between his fingers. The author's tape-recorder can be seen next to the '555' pack.

RDB's Fiat Car - BMC 1139, which he loved to drive at high speeds.

11 days before he passed away, Panchamda commented that 'BMC' stands for 'Best Music Composer' !

Rekha chats with the author at the 'Agar Tum Na Hote' party — where RDB could not make it.

RDB chatting with the author at the 'Dil Padosi Hai' album launch party.

Author posing with R D Burman at the 'Pantera' album release party.
Note the stressed look on RDB's face, as there was a lukewarm market response to the Latino-American album.

Courtesy: Anand-Milind

'Qayamat Se QayamatTak' music release event where 'mascot' R D Burman was the 'chief guest.' Hero Aamir Khan can be seen standing next to RDB, back row, center.

Courtesy: Ranjit Gazmer

RDB with his Dream Team of musicians – *Tera saath na chhodenge.*

Courtesy: Suneil Anand Navketan Films

Glam-diva Zeenat Aman with Dev Anand in the hippie anthem Dum Maro Dum.'

Pele postage stamp, 1969

"Enthusiasm is everything. It must be taut and vibrating like a guitar string" – **Pele** (refer page 37)

Rhythm master Burjor Lord – he played the drums for the iconic songs 'Dum maro dum' and 'I love you'

R.D. Burman's Stamp And R.D. Burman Striking A Pose On The Synthesizers. This picture on the right was clicked by the author in 1983; refer Chapter 8: Indelible Stamp of Genius.

RDB and Mehmood in a working still from 'Bhoot Bungla.'

Courtesy: Rajshri

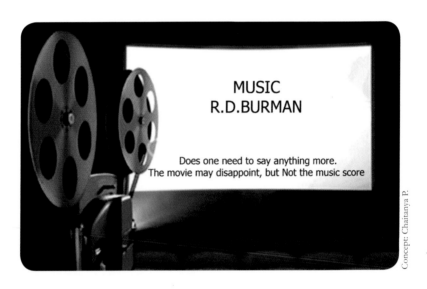

MUSIC
R.D.BURMAN

Does one need to say anything more.
The movie may disappoint, but Not the music score

Concept: Chaitanya P.

PART 3

Glowing Sentimental Tributes to RDB
from Luminaries & Celebs

'Bharat Ratna'—Lata Mangeshkar

Supreme 'Numero Uno' Legendary Playback Singer
Who Has Enthralled the Masses, Globally,
for Over Seven Decades

'Besides the large number of solos and duets, I have also sung three songs with Pancham as my 'co-singer' in movies like 'Libaas,' 'Ek Se Bhale Do' and in 'Hare Rama Hare Krishna.' It was such a mirthful experience working with a talented composer who would take so much effort to brief me on 'what exactly he wanted' in every song. Occasionally he would let me improvise, but most of the time he would sing and rehearse with me, before we went for the final take. Since he called me 'Didi' and considered me like his elder sister, he would treat me with fond reverential respect. Not just classical gems like 'Raina beeti jaaaye' or 'Naam Goom Jaayega,' but the versatile Rahul made me sing a wide range of contrasting genres of tracks. For that endearing number 'Baahon mein chali aao,' RDB insisted that I should sing it in low-pitched soft tones to match the romantic mood of that track. Observe the way, he made me beautifully stretch that word 'Aaaaaaoo.' In that musical hit film 'Caravan,' I sang both 'Chadti jawaani meri chaal mastani' and 'Dilbar dil se pyare dilbar' which heroine Aruna Irani performed so well on screen. For that song 'Dilbar ' Pancham discussed with me, that he wanted me to sing in a slightly rough, sultry yet mellifluous way. Because it was a 'gypsy-song.' It was to be picturised on a coquettish, tomboyish banjaaran girl (Aruna). It was commendable, the way RDB made me sing that phrase 'nainonwaale' in five different variations while shifting scales. Due credit also goes to lyricist Majrooh-saab for his classy lyrics.

One of my favorite unusual RDB songs is the raga-fusion song 'Aisa samaa na hota' and the beautiful 'Tere liye palkon ke jhaalar bunoo.' These films apparently did not create huge waves at the box-office. But these songs which I have sung are still so heart-warming.

When Pancham got married, he told me, 'Didi, I don't want any expensive gift from you. Instead write me a counselling 'letter' on the do's and don'ts of life, and how to lead a blissful married life.' I did so, and I believe he had carefully preserved that letter in his 'locker.'

One of my biggest regrets of my singing career is that when I sang his 'Kuchh na kaho,' Pancham had already passed away. During 93, I remember one young man came to convey the message that 'R. D. Burman wanted to record one song in my voice. Then Pancham-da himself called me and said 'Didi, I need your voice, for this particular song—and only your voice.' Unfortunately I had to tell Pancham—'not now, *"kyunki main USA jaa rahin hoon, live concerts ke liye"* and after I return, you may book the recording studio'. After I returned to India, I had to rush to Delhi for some urgent work. And there on 4 January 1994, I heard the shocking news that Pancham-da was no more.

All of us were very upset, but we had to fulfil Pancham's last music-related wish. In early February '94, we recorded the song 'Kucch na kaho' at the Western Outdoor Studios, and I remember that Sanjeev Kohli handled the recording, and Sanjay Leela Bhansali was also present there.

Had RDB been alive, I am sure he may have made some 'extempore' changes in my song and perhaps made it sound even 'better.' This recording was one of my most challenging as Pancham's fond memories kept recurring in my mind. Although I was not keeping too well, with a sense of anguish in my heart, I completed the song.

My message to all RDB fans is that, although he left us abruptly at a young age, **the musical charisma of his songs and unique voice will always be remembered and cherished for generations to come.** *"Aise mahaan sangeetkar-gaayak Pancham ka naam, kabhi goom nahin jaayega, balki hamesha dhoom machaayega."*

'Padma Vibhushan' ASHA BHOSLE

THE LEGENDARY EVERGREEN MELODY QUEEN

'Most Bollywood composers are self-confessed die-hard fans of R. D. Burman. That could be the reason, why every third song that one hears has the fleeting jhalak of Pancham's signature style. Some new music directors, have even said that, they have the 'hangover' of having grown up, listening to RDB's hit songs, so they have a tough time, trying 'not' to be influenced by them.

As a person, Pancham was not at all attached to luxurious or materialistic possessions. For him, musical notes symbolized the *'keemti khazaana.'* Once when I showed him my new diamond ring, he said, *'Oh achcha,* this is how a diamond looks' and shrugged his attention within seconds to new tune that he was toying with. Luxury cars would hardly fascinate him, he would prefer driving his own modest cosy Fiat unto the last.

Gaana, non-veg khaana aur khaana pakaana, these were 'Bub's (RDB) three prime passions. Besides experimenting in Western and Hindustani music, we both shared a common passion of 'cooking' at home. **There used to be a constant 'one-upmanship' between us as to who is the 'better'** *gharelu baawarchi.*

Generally speaking, he would conjure up the more complex and difficult tunes for me, because he had the 'confidence' that I could do take up the challenge and do full justice to it. And I would live up to his confidence. **The experimental RDB made me sing the sensuous** cabaret number 'Aaj ki raat koi'. Then in total contrast in the same movie 'Anamika,' I also recorded the devotional track 'Jaaoon toh kaahan jaaoon' with equal ease. The iconic 'Aaja aaja, main hoon pyar tera' (Teesri Manzil) was quite a difficult song and he was delighted, when I gave my very best to that song. **When as a playback singer, I won prestigious awards for awesome tracks such as 'Dum maro dum,' 'Mera kuchh saamaan,' and 'Piya tu ab toh aaja,' the credit for such fabulous 'compositions' also indirectly goes to RDB.** We worked quite hard on that classical song 'Piya Baawre' (Khubsoorat) and see how well the song turned out. Way back in the past, there were times when a couple of cynical producers who were carried away by his 'Westernized' image, wrongly felt maybe Pancham was incapable of giving classical gems like his legendary father Sachin-da. There were rare occasions when RDB was compelled to use his presence of mind, and tell such skeptical producers, that it was his father's tune, when actually it was he who had composed that same song.

'Bubs' was more of a good friend, impulsive, unpredictable at times with fickle moods. Despite the absence of MTV in India, during those days, he was conversant with latest 'world music' by listening to cassettes and records. Monotony would put him off, while polyphony would turn him on. **At times he had a freakish sense of humour, quite child-like.** On my *janamdin*, as many already know, he once presented me a gift-wrapped 'broom' along with a rose. Only because, I am so obsessive about cleanliness.

The greatest testimony to Pancham's timeless talent is that wherever and whenever his chartbuster songs are played or performed 'live,' there is such an overwhelming sentimental response. **The unconditional love of his loyal fans is what mattered to him the most.'**

The Author has interacted with this iconic singer on multiple occasions including her 'live' concerts in Mumbai, the RDB memorial chowk inaugural event(2009), at Poonam Dhillon's birthday party and during her film 'Mai' (2013) promotional events.

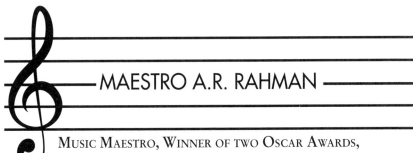

MAESTRO A.R. RAHMAN

MUSIC MAESTRO, WINNER OF TWO OSCAR AWARDS,
TWO GRAMMY AWARDS, FOUR NATIONAL AWARDS,
MULTIPLE FILMFARE AWARDS AND THE FILMFARE
R D BURMAN AWARD FOR NEW MUSIC TALENT (IN 1995)

'Every generation a rebel is born to make our lives more colorful. Mr. R. D. Burman was that for me, from that generation'

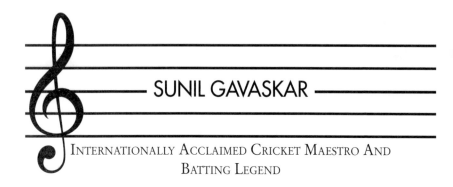

SUNIL GAVASKAR

INTERNATIONALLY ACCLAIMED CRICKET MAESTRO AND
BATTING LEGEND

'He came on the music scene like a breath of fresh air. While Hindi film music then seemed more about orchestras with violins, RDB brought the guitar into play and got young India hooked to his music. **'Teesri Manzil' was the first foray and a turning point of sorts in Hindi film music. That my favourite, the one and only, Shammi Kapoor was the one dancing in his own inimitable style to RDB's music made it even more memorable.**

RDB came up with new tunes for every film that he scored the music for and he blew everyone's minds with those unforgettable songs in Amar Prem, Aap Ki Kasam and many more.

Who would have thought that the man who brought the guitar strumming in Hindi music with the numbers in 'Teesri Manzil,' 'Hare Rama Hare Krishna' could also give you the soft lilting songs in 'Amar Prem' and 'Aap Ki Kasam.'

Am sure that the Gods above were starving for good music and so took him away from us at such a young age'

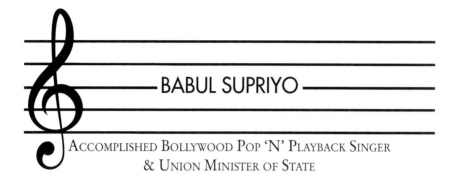

BABUL SUPRIYO

Accomplished Bollywood Pop 'N' Playback Singer & Union Minister of State

'**R**.D. Burman's repertoire has no 'expiry date' because his 'futuristic' songs have already conquered hearts across three generations. With their youthful global appeal and contemporary relevance, his retro songs actually don't need to be 'remixed.' **Like 'Chaplinesque,' the term 'Panchamazing' can now be used as an adjective, describing benchmark musical talent. What a charged battery is to a cell-phone, singing RDB songs is to me—it gives me the power and energy.** If I get the opportunity, someday I would love to initiate an RDB music training school and probably name it 'RDX' as students can also discover their own 'X-factor.''

ILLUSTRIOUS LUMINARIES

'The iconic music director, the late R. D. Burman, who was arguably one of the best music directors of Hindi cinema for over two decades. Until death snatched him away, when he was at the peak of his career.'

—**Shyam Benegal,** Internationally acclaimed veteran film-maker

'I profusely thank Mrs. Meera Burman and Mr. Sachin Dev Burman for giving birth to an immortal musician, composer-singer known as the one-and-only Rahul Dev Burman. Yes, he made an exit too soon, but he will be the one who will live infinitely long. Love you Pancham-da!'

– **Sachin Pilgaonkar**
Proficient prolific actor, film-maker and music-savvy singer

'Pancham-da had music not only in his name but also in his genes. **Like most geniuses, unfortunately, we have realized his worth only after he passed away.** I was very lucky to have spent time with him and have him give amazing songs in so many of my popular films including 'Red Rose,' 'Yeh Vaada Raha,' 'Biwi-O-Biwi,' 'Baseraa,' 'Samundar,' 'Sitamgar' etc.'

– **Poonam Dhillon,**
Versatile Bollywood star-actress with a smart 'music sense'

'Though I've listened to R. D. Burman all my life, 'Beeti naa beetayi raina' from 'Parichay' is the first song I recognized as his. **Panchamda's music is timeless and connects with people across generations.** I also love the Bengali song 'Deke deke koto' which RDB himself sang. When he sang, it felt like he was speaking in tune. It was that effortless!'

– Vidya Balan
Music connoisseur and National Award-winning actress.

'As a kid I often heard the cult song 'Duniya mein logon ko'; this voice was different, and I fell in love with the energy of this voice. That's where my RDB connect began. In college, our group of boys would sing 'Yeh jawani, hai diwani,' although Hrithik's 'Ek pal ka jeena' had already gripped the fancy of the nation. When I started my retro-music radio show as a popular RJ, I discovered that out of the ten retro songs that I loved, at least eight of them were RDB compositions. That's when I dived into his sea of music and also the mystique of Pancham, the man. Even today on my radio show, the majority of the songs I play are melodious RDB tracks—they reach across all generations. *Pancham amar hai!*'

– **Anmol Sood, eminent and popular RJ**

'R. D. Burman-Sir is one of India's most prolific composers who changed the game when it came to innovative Bollywood music in that golden era. Winning the RDB Filmfare Award will always remain my most special memory. It comes with a huge responsibility, and I will try my best to fulfill that. Too many great songs of RDB to select a favorite, but on top of my mind is the melodious 'Naam gum jaayega.'

– **Siddharth (Shankar) Mahadevan**
Excellent singer and recipient of Filmfare R. D. Burman New Music Talent Award, 2014

'RDB is not just a huge influence on Vishal-Shekhar, the most rocking musical duo of the decade, but is pretty much an ageless legendary musician because of the sounds he created anew for every song he composed. His soul was very deep and understood all aspects of music. Besides, he had a strong opinion because of which his music was individualistic and unique. His ability to live every moment 'completely' is what made him an inventive genius in his style of music.'

– Archana Pania

Popular Radio Jockey

'He (R. D. Burman) was never *not* working. He worked when he was travelling, talking, listening, eating, drinking (including tea), watching football, midnight driving, dreaming—except that it wasn't work for him.

And it was pure joy for the rest of the world.

'*Aap log mera age wrong bataate ho. I'm still growing up,*' said RDB, just a couple of months before he permanently stopped growing.'

– Harish Bhimani

National Award-winning voice-over artiste and acclaimed compere

'Late' Superstar RAJESH KHANNA

'RD FOR ME MEANT ROMANTIC DIE-HARD':
LATE SUPERSTAR RAJESH KHANNA,
WHO WAS RDB'S CLOSE BUDDY.

Erstwhile superstar Rajesh Khanna, who has acted in some thirty-four movies whose music has been scored by R. D. Burman was a very close buddy of the late classy composer. Since I knew 'Kaka-ji' (Khanna's nickname in showbiz) very well, he had invited me on the sets of one of his under-productions. My meeting with the Khanna was on 30 Dec, just a day after his birthday. The 'spot-boy' dedicated to the former matinee-idol got us tangy orange-juice in glass mugs and a plateful of crisp biscuits and a few pastries. Four days later, fans all over would religiously observe the fifteenth death anniversary of the illustrious Pancham-da. As I prodded him to waltz into a flashback, the optimistic Khanna refused to lament on the untimely death of the fifty-four-year-old melody master. The temperamental yet optimistic Khanna countered with, 'Who says R. D. Burman is 'no more.' *Hum toh kehte hain ki aaj bhi Pancham hamare saath hain. Bilkul zinda hain rey,* thru his legacy of chartbuster music. *Dekhne jaaye toh,* after he passed away, there are these huge waves of music lovers wanting to 'know more' about the genius behind his repertoire. The phenomenon called Pancham-da can never die, because his repertoire of evergreen, futuristic songs keeps him alive and rocking. We were more like soulmates– made for each other.

Although we did have our share of bitter arguments and frivolous fights, there would soon be a cordial 'ceasefire.' Whenever I'm listening to his snappy or soulful numbers, I feel I'm 'with him,'" insists Khanna as he tilts his head and almost crinkles his eyes. What made him feel that today's fickle-minded, fastidious, fast-forward generation would get easily hooked on to the 'Pancham-mania'? Stormed the 'Kati Patang' hero, 'The other day, when I happened to watch a group of young boys and girls swaying to the recycled version of the hit 'Bachna ae haseenon' smartly reprised by Vishal & Shekhar, originally composed by Rahul, three decades ago, I was ecstatic to observe that the next generation was already allured by Pied Piper Pancham (chuckles). Even Shah Rukh Khan's 'Main Hoon Naa' directed by the music-savvy Farah Khan had frequent background tunes of vintage RDB scores. Which is why I constantly feel his 'presence' through his timeless music,' elaborates Kaka.

Not surprisingly, Khanna admits that Pancham-da was 'instrumental' in his take-off to stardom. 'With all due respect to his music maestro father Sachin Dev Burman, the legendary number 'Mere sapnon ki rani' in 'Aradhana' was partially the brain-wave of his talented son. Because I witnessed the song being 'born' during the sittings. Since Pancham-da himself played the harmonica, he has incorporated peppy portions of harmonica melodies in that song just before Kishore-da butts in with Ae hey hey hey lara lara la.

Wasn't it true that Burman Junior composed most of his chartbuster tunes at unearthly hours and in unconventional situations? 'That's right. At times, he would even 'dream' of a melody and jot down the notations when he woke up. Just about any bizarre sound would inspire him. From a discordant car honking to an ear-splitting aircraft drone could inspire him. Once, Pancham and I were flying together to Delhi for the premiere of 'Baharon Ke Sapne.' When the plane took off and started cruising, he started humming a catchy tune. The moment I heard it, I cajoled him to use it for one of my playback songs.

Months later, we were at the 'sitting' of 'Kati Patang' and we just could not get the right tune for a particular song which had a waltz metre. That's when, fortunately, I could recall the same tune that RDB had sung at 32,000 feet. This melody, which was instantly approved by director Shakti-da Samanta, was none other than 'Yeh jo mohabbat hai' which always literally gives me a 'high' because of the high altitude that it was originally hummed.'

Even the devotional music at a temple was yet another inspirational trigger? 'Absolutely right. We were at a Shivji Mandir-darshan somewhere in Kashmir. After listening to the clanging of temple bells and rhythmic pounding of drums during the aarti, we came out. Within maybe 45 seconds, RDB instantly hummed a dummy devotional hook line with a folksy beat. This time, he assured me that he would 'gift' the melody to me. Many months later, that vibrant tune was recorded as the famous duet 'Jai jai shiv shankar' from the movie 'Aap Ki Kasam.' Many a time, he would use the whistle-effect or la-la-la in some of his songs as he felt that the common man could whistle his melodies, even without memorizing the lyrics,' recalls Khanna.

Would the 'Amar Prem' hero recall how the iconic song 'Duniya Mein' came into being? 'After a few sips of his orange juice, he jogs into a flashback. 'When he had first sung 'Meri jaan maine kahaa' in his grunting bass voice for my movie 'The Train' (1970), I was fascinated with that unconventional Pancham voice. After we became close, he promised me that someday in future he would give 'sing' a memorable landmark playback number which I would lip-sync to. It materialized two years later when I signed on for 'Apna Desh' which was a Hindi adaptation of the 1969 Tamil superhit 'Nam Naadu' (which also means 'apna desh'). There is a similar situation in the Tamil movie where the hero and heroine are masquerading and trying to hoodwink the villains. But the Southside playback singer (T. M. Soundararajan) has sung that song ('Ninathathai nadathiyae') in a normal voice. But being super-innovative RDB decided to use his rasp bass and even disguise his voice. Because his logic was that if you are in outlandish disguise even your awaaz should not be recognized. And then the mukhda went 'Logon ko dhokaa kabhi ho jaata hai.' While I was not too sure how the audiences would react to the freakish rasps with all the breath-taking gasps, Pancham was confident that the song would jolt the audiences and reach cultish proportions. Otherwise which composer-singer would have the gutsy conviction to make a mega-star like me 'lip-sync' to bizarre vocal gimmicks,' smiles Khanna who has also lip-synced to Pancham-da's normal mellifluous voice for this Bengali duet 'Madhobi futchi oi' (the 'Baagon mein bahaar hai' counterpart) from the Bengali version of Aradhana. 'Since one is used to RDB's vocal gimmicks, this Bengali song in Pancham's normal dulcet voice equally bowls you over, as a rare gem,' he points out.

Wasn't the moody RDB initially reluctant to score the title music of Kaka-ji's first-ever home-production TV serial titled *Aadha Sach Aadha Jhooth*' **(1987)?** 'That's quite true, because a slightly peeved Pancham said he did not want to jump on the TV serial bandwagon. But then, I told him, in that case I would perhaps 'drop' the TV project if he backed out. That's when he relented and even 'sang' the gimmicky title song. After a couple of chorus retakes, the track was finally approved by the overall discerning talented TV serial director Tarun Mathur. But Pancham's voice was the lucky charm of the serial,' insists the Khanna. The former superstar, who remained fast friends with Pancham-da, disagrees with the popular notion that RDB was always a recluse. 'Basically, Rahul was a shy, sensitive, reserved person who never grabbed media mileage. As a human being, he was very jolly, witty and fun-loving. The milestone song 'Ek chatur naar' (Padosan), which is a classical-pop freak-fusion, bears testimony to his humorous flip side.'

'Besides being a die-hard romantic at heart, he romanticised life, which is how he could create mushy serenading songs like 'Jaane-jaan' (Jawani Diwani), 'Chura liya hai tumne' (Yaadon Ki Baarat) and 'Hum dono do premi' (Ajnabee),' counters Kaka, who deeply regrets that his close buddy had to go through a luckless, depressing phase post 1991, when the showbiz industry 'disowned' him as his music was 'no longer saleable.'

'Ruthless destiny snatched him away just when he was ready to start his second innings with his brilliant score in Vidhu Vinod Chopra's '1942: A Love Story.' Although we have some fabulous singer-composers today, none, I feel, can match up to RDB's extraordinary calibre,' Kaka said, sighing.

Finally, fifteen years after his untimely demise in 1994, a memorial 'chowk' at Santacruz, West, close to Pancham-da's residence, was named after him and was unveiled by Gulzar and Asha Bhonsle on 4 Jan 2009. This memorial was all thanks to the initiative taken by a group of dedicated RDB fans from Pune, who diligently run a popular Panchammagic Fans' association. 'We need many more such dedicated memorial junctions and functions, music academies and loyal fan clubs to revive the 'punch' of Pancham-da's repertoire for all times to come,' signs off Khanna.

Rajesh Khanna's Top 10 favourite R. D. Burman songs

- Zindagi ke safar mein (Aap Ki Kasam)
- Duniya mein (Apna Desh)
- Oh mere dil ke chain (Mere Jeevan Saathi)
- Chingari koi bhadke (Amar Prem)
- Humein tumse pyar kitna (Kudrat)
- Ek chatur naar (Padosan)
- Dum maro dum (Hare Rama Hare Krishna)
- Hum bewafaa hargiz na they (Shalimar)
- Jaane-e-jaan (Jawani Diwani)
- Baahon mein chali aa (Anamika)

 Director RAMESH SIPPY (of 'Sholay' fame)!·

'Undoubtedly, the legendary duo Shankar Jaikishan had given a memorable classy score for my directorial debut 'Andaaz' (1971). When I was planning my next movie 'Seeta Aur Geeta,' Jaikishan had passed away, and I was faced with a dilemma as to whom should I approach. **Music is like the soul of any feature film.** There were multiple choices of leading composers.

Coincidentally, I happened to hear this song 'Sharabi tera naam' from the movie 'Chandan Ka Palna' (1967), which was picturised on an 'inebriated' Meena Kumari. Not only was the track sung by Lata-ji very appealing, but it had 'syncopated' rhythm beats to match the tipsy mood and of the song. This was something very innovative, I felt. When I checked the credits, I realized it was composed by R. D. Burman. That was the deciding factor and in no time we had finalized Pancham for 'Seeta Aur Geeta'(1972).

It's a bizarre yet pleasant coincidence that even in 'Seeta' there was a situation where heroine Hema Malini is also shown 'tipsy.' And RDB brilliantly composed 'Haan jee haan, maine sharaab pee hai.' Once again, legendary Lata-ji sang the track to 'bossa nova' rhythm beats.

There used to be wrong perception about R. D. Burman that he was too much into heavy Western rhythm percussion and his Indian melody sense was not as good as that of his father, Sachin-da. In my films, he exploded that myth. **When we signed him for 'Sholay,' he** was terribly excited when he heard the subject. With stereophonic sound facilities, he was all the more enthusiastic. Not only the songs but even the background instrumental scores emerged an all-time landmark. RD was emotionally optimistic even before the release.

What a command and mastery he had over both Indian classical and folk and Western harmonies. Even after four decades, the 'Sholay' Indo-Western fusion credit titles masterpiece is a mandatory must at every RDB Memorial 'live' concert. And so is 'Mehbooba mehbooba,' where Pancham was nominated by Filmfare in the 'Best Playback' singer category. For that matter, except one, all our home-banner movies which have RDB's music ('Sholay,' 'Shaan' and 'Saagar') have also been 'nominated' in the Filmfare 'Best Music Direction' category. Regardless of their box-office-performance, his songs for our home-banner movies 'Shaan' and 'Saagar' have been ever-crisp chartbusters. What an innovative sense of background music RDB had is evident in 'Sholay'—whether it was the dreaded Gabbar Singh's eerie entry or the soothing harmonica piece played by Amitabh.

The reason we decided to have the song 'Mehbooba' as a solo and not a duet is because we wished to be 'different.' Isn't it unique to see the graceful Helen not doing a lip-sync in a seductive dance number? And that modest genius meticulously did it all with a flourish. My long association with Pancham was a fusion of *kaam-dosti-aur-pyaar* and we shared lots of jubilant moments even on the personal front. With his zany sense of humour and zestful energy levels, he had this genuine sense of constant curiosity and restlessness, which I felt was very 'child-like.' But he also had a great deal of maturity in handling his work and his team.

It was a distinguished honour working with RDB, and I shall always cherish every moment of my creative camaraderie with him.'—

– Director Ramesh Sippy (of 'Sholay' fame)!

AMEEN SAYANI

VETERAN 'PAR EXCELLENCE' RADIO JOCKEY AND COMPERE

Sureelay raag ho ya dhoom-dhaam - Pancham ne roshan kar diya apna naam

'I began to know Pancham when he was a sprightly young schoolboy in shorts. Every time I visited Dada Burmans' house, I used to see young Pancham rhythmically shaking while his hands played on tablas or bongos. His whole 'restless' body would also often sway to some unseen imaginary 'beats,' whenever he was in a merry musical mood.

And then Pancham flowered out as a most 'unusual' composer on his own. His first official offering was 'Chhote Nawab.' It was a beautiful number of his from that film—'Ghar aaja ghir aaye'—that helped to break a two year old deadlock between Dada Burman and Lata Mangeshkar. When Pancham sang the composition to Dada, he immediately rang Lata up, and said, 'Lata, my son Pancham is becoming a music director, and he has composed a beautiful song that you alone could give justice to. Will you sing it?' And Lata replied, 'Dada, when you have asked me to sing it, how can I say 'no'?' And that's how the long tension between two great music legends—Dada and Lata—came to an end, and she again sang countless lovely songs for Dada thereafter!

Versatile Pancham's music always had an undertone of rich Indian raga-based melody. But he also created hundreds of numbers decorated with the unmatched *"dhoom dhaam"* of highly Westernised melody and rhythm.

He became one of India's most lovable music directors—even though fate took him away at quite a young age. He was just fifty-four when he died. The world of retro music lovers will miss him forever.'

"One of the tragedies of real life is, that there is no background music."

– Annie Proulx, 'The Shipping News' Book –1993

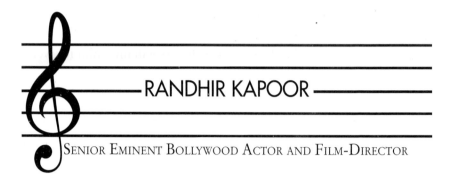

RANDHIR KAPOOR

SENIOR EMINENT BOLLYWOOD ACTOR AND FILM-DIRECTOR

Not many are aware that it was none other than actor-director Randhir 'Dabboo' Kapoor who accepted the 'posthumous' Filmfare Award for Best Music Director in 1995 for 'late' R. D. Burman, for his masterpiece score for the movie '1942: A Love Story' directed by Vidhu Vinod Chopra. Explains Randhir, 'That's simply because I shared a close bonding with my best buddy Pancham. Since Asha-ji Bhosle knew that, she graciously insisted that I should publicly collect his Filmfare Award on stage. And that precious trophy still lies in my safe custody' revealed the senior Kapoor when I met him, in his spacious cabin, which has classic vintage portraits adorning the walls, at the iconic R. K. Studios at Chembur.

The unassuming Kapoor, whose 'diva' star-daughters Karishma and Kareena, are frequently making media headlines, prefers watching latest movies with the actual audience, at nearby premium cinema theatres. Jogging into a Burmanesque flashback, the 'cricket connoisseur' Randhir is frank enough to declare that 'RDB was instrumental in boosting my acting career. With his 'sheer genius' he gifted me with 'Jawani Diwani,' 'Rampur ka Lakshman' and many more including 'Kasme Vaade' and 'Rickshawala' which had brilliant scores. We had a common dear friend the 'late' Ramesh 'Gogi' Behl who produced *Jawani Diwani.'* In fact RDB has even given 'playback' for me in this foot-tapping yet meaningful song 'Kal Kya Hoga Kisko Pata' ('Kasme Vaade').

Once we became best of buddies, RDB was my obvious choice for our RK banner venture 'Dharam Karam' (1975) which I also directed. In which he gave us amazing songs especially the Mukesh number 'Ek din bik jaayega.' My music-savvy dad Raj Kapoor appreciated Pancham's compositions for its distinct style,' he smiles wistfully.

Post 'pack-up,' wasn't RDB known for his fetish for good food? With a hearty chuckle, the RK scion recalls, 'Not just eating, maestro Pancham who also had a witty sense of humour was an excellent cook. After my late-night sessions with him, he would affectionately cook delicious non-vegetarian food for us. While the rest of us would be busy sipping drinks, RDB would be busy with his *'khaana pakaana'* whilst humming some *vilayti or desi dhun.* We would end up spending together at least three to four 'late nights' in a week.'reveals the senior Kapoor.

What exactly was that *'kissa'* about him eventually getting his much-desired song-tune in 'Harjaee'? Smiles Randhir, 'At one of the 'sittings,' RDB hummed a catchy tune which I instantly got hooked onto. But being ethical, he initially refused to grant me that tune for my songs, as he had already 'committed' it to some other leading film-maker. Much later, that film was 'shelved' and luckily Pancham incorporated that same tune for the song 'Tujhsa Haseen' in my movie 'Harjaee' (1981), which is among my top favourites,' shrugs the candid Kapoor who appeared peeved and furious over the remixes of the all-time classic RDB hippie anthem 'Dum maro dum.' **'Anyone who 'murders' RDB's original iconic songs should be publicly flogged and can never be forgiven,' reacts Randhir in an outburst of emotional anger.**

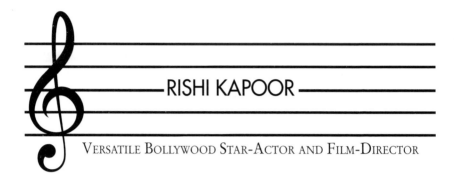

RISHI KAPOOR

Evergreen Bollywood actor Rishi Kapoor can converse non-stop for hours together on his favourite buddy-composer Rahul Dev Burman. 'Today's filmy songs barely have a recall-life of '31 days.' Against that, the iconic hit R. D. Burman number 'Bachna ae haseeno' picturised on me in 1977 re-emerged as a chartbusting remix encore thirty-one years later, in 2008 when it was picturised on my actor-son Ranbir. It's a unique film-music benchmark that celebrates Rahul-da's timeless talent,' he says with a glow of pride on his face.

The innovative Pancham would zestfully compose for Rishi, because he felt that the latter would add both *"jaan aur shaan"* to the on-screen songs with his agile dancing. Reacts the outspoken Kapoor, 'That's so humbling. Since I also attended Pancham's song recordings and sittings he seemed to derive delight composing for me. We would even indulge in banter and even hyper-arguments. Knowing my in-born sense of music, 'Dada' even got me to hum vocal support lyrics along with the legendary Kishore-da who was the main singer, for the track 'Dil mein jo mere samaa' (Jhoota Kahin Ka). It's among my favourites, especially since it reminds you of the 'Chalti Ka Naam Gaadi' songs, because it's shot in a garage with car mechanics indulging in funny antics and weird sounds. Then I also contributed vocal support for the title-song and for 'Poochho na yaar kya hua' from 'Zamaane Ko Dikhana Hai'.'

'Frankly speaking, I never considered myself a great dancer, so due credit also goes to the wonderful rhythm of RDB's songs and all the dedicated dance-masters. But I was always passionate about giving perfect expressions during the songs. The reason why Pancham's vibrant chartbusters picturised on me are evergreen is because they were young and vibrant. Back then, I was the youngest lover-boy on the star-block. Besides, he would brilliantly use 'bass-guitar' strumming in my songs which infectiously connected with the collegians. Some of my movies like 'Dhan Daulat' were not hits at the box-office. But they all had amazing songs by RDB. That is to say, I may have failed at the box-office, but Pancham's music would never fail me,' he asserts.

Wasn't it true that this popular energetic song 'Ruk jaana O jaana' from 'Warrant' picturised on Dev Anand, was supposedly composed by RDB keeping Rishi in mind? 'Oh yes, its sheer bad luck that Dev-saab who 'overheard' the song being sung in the sitting-room was so enamoured, that he was adamant that Pancham should record it for his upcoming movie. As they say, *gaane-gaane pey likkha hai adaa karne wale ka naam,*' chuckles the Kapoor ruefully.

The exuberant Chintu is sentimental about 'Dil lena khel hai' which Burman had sang for him in his 'high octave' voice. 'During the studio-shoot of this song which has RDB's electronic wizardry, Pancham would personally drop in to cheer me up. And while he was munching a '*paan,*' I would jestfully jibe at him gazing at me, whether he thought I was a '*kothewaali*' dancer,' laughs Chintu who fondly remembers the *taareef* showered on him by the composer. 'Dada used to compliment me for 'convincingly' playing the guitar and trumpet on-screen. Especially since I don't know to play any musical instruments. These days, it's disheartening, when certain contemporary 'hit-and-run' songs with no lyrical value, seem to function mainly as brief caller-tunes. We miss your musical genius, Dada,' sighs the outspoken Kapoor.

Five RDB-Rishi musical milestone movies:

Khel Khel Mein, Hum Kisi Se Kum Nahin, Zamane Ko Dikhana Hai, Yeh Vaada Raha, Saagar.

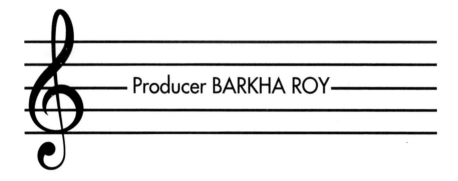

Producer BARKHA ROY

'**P**anchamda initially refused to believe that he had finally bagged his first-ever Filmfare Award**'** discloses producer Barkha Roy (former leading Bollywood heroine Reena Roy's sister).

It was in her musical jubilee hit film 'Sanam Teri Kasam' (1982) that the late legendary composer R. D. Burman won his first-ever Filmfare Award after being in showbiz for over two decades. Exclusive tribute from producer Barkha Roy, as told to the author Chaitanya Padukone

'When I started off in 1982 as a bubbly young producer with 'Sanam Teri Kasam(STK),' R. D. Burman was already an established top-ranking music director who had dozens of mega-hits like 'Teesri Manzil,' 'Padosan,' 'Caravan,' 'Bombay to Goa,' 'Jawani Diwani' and of course 'Sholay.' Being a young beginner, as compared to the bigwigs, I was small fry. During the music sittings of the 'Jaane jaan o meri…' song, I vividly recall Pancham using the dummy lyrics word 'Zia… zia… zia.' That's when I butted in and said, why use some strange name when it has nothing to do with my movie. Instead I suggested to Pancham that we should use 'Nisha' because that was the name of the 'lead character' which my sister Reena Roy was playing. During this 'Jaana o meri jaana' song sitting, RDB was keen on approaching Kishore-da to record the song. But after hearing Pancham-da sing the tune so beautifully with such passion, I insisted that he record it in his own normal voice minus any of his 'patented' grating raspy vocals. On an impulse he said, 'but, you will have to pay me Rs. 10,000/-.' But since I was adamant, I instantly countered by saying that I would give him Rs. 12000/-. We both then had a hearty laugh. Besides being a genius innovative composer, he had streaks of creativity even for song picturisation. Till this day, I vividly remember that Pancham-da dropped in on the studio-sets whilst we were shooting 'Jaana o meri jaana' which he had sung. After observing for a while he suggested that whilst hero Kamal Haasan was playing the trumpet, during the song interlude, his beret cap should be shown levitating and dancing in the air, before it fell on his head. We incorporated Dada's brilliant suggestion. And it's there as a visual delight in that song for all times to come. Even for 'Jaane jaan' in 'Nisha,' I compelled Panchamda to sing that initial refrain phrase. And his voice beautifully blended with the rest of the racy number sung sensuously with the 'vibrato-quiver' vocal by the inimitable Asha-ji Bhosle. Keeping in mind that Reena is a trained classical dancer, Pancham incorporated the tabla beats in *Dhin thinak dhin*' in the mukhda. In fact, after our whole movie was complete and after we got our censor certificate, I coaxed RDB to compose a eleventh hour, add-on waltzy number as I am very fond of waltz beats. And my guardian-angel that he was, he fulfilled my wish by composing the waltz beat song 'Sheeshey ke gharon mein.' And guess what, he instantly agreed. After 'STK' released, we were overwhelmed with the audience responses to the chartbuster score by RDB, particularly the 'Jaane jaan oh meri jaanaa,' dance number sung by Asha Bhonsle with the initial vocal notes hummed by Pancham-da himself.

When the time came to send the Filmfare Award nominations, RDB seemed highly cynical and stormed *paagal ho gayi kya*—we can't even dream of bringing home the award,' That's because he felt that, if his superlative music scores for movies like 'Amar Prem,' 'Teesri Manzil,' 'Hare Rama Hare Krishna,' 'Caravan,' 'Parichay,' 'Kati Patang' and 'Mere Jeevan Saathi' had bitterly lost out, over the past two decades, 'Sanam Teri Kasam' would hardly stand any chance. So he left the entire decision to me. *'Agar tujhme hosh aur josh hai to* 'Sanam Teri Kasam' ka nomination bhej do, lekin mujhe bilkul hopes nahin," he said on a pessimistic note. Ultimately, the results were announced and I informed him that 'STK' had won the Filmfare Award for the 'Best Music' score. He initially refused to believe it! There were mixed feelings of pent-up anger, ecstasy and disbelief. But that night, he later told me, he shed tears of joy like a little kid, because in the process, he had also fulfilled his 'late' dad Sachin-da's long-awaited dream.

Besides 'STK,' we worked together for two more movies 'Karishma' and 'Gunhegaar Kaun.' Contrary to false rumours, my movie 'Karishma' (1984) was successfully released. But the rocking music scored by RDB was not marketed properly. Even today if you listen to the mind-blowing rhythmic frenzy song 'Ek haseen gulbadan' sung by Panchamda in his normal voice, you will freak out. When I signed RDB for 'Gunhegaar Kaun' (1991), he was in his downslide phase when almost all his top-banner regular producers had drastically 'deserted' him. Jokingly he would say, after my 'cardiac by-pass,' the producers have by-passed me but *mera music mere 'aas-pass' hai, woh mujhe chhod kar kahin nahin jaayega.* Music companies curtly told me to 'replace him with a more saleable name.' But I stuck to my guns and preferred to go ahead with Burman-da's music score. Nobody, I feel, can ever 'replace' a divine *karishma* called Rahul Dev Burman. And I am positively sure, that lakhs of his die-hard fans will agree with me. Salaam Pancham-da, both you and your magic melodies are immortal and forever.'

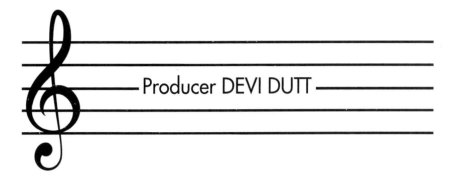

Producer DEVI DUTT

Eminent producer **Devi Dutt** *(legendary Guru Dutt's younger brother) feels that, the heart-break and disillusionment pangs that Pancham-da went thru, when Guru Dutt's 'Raaz' failed to take off, stands vindicated. That's because twenty-five years later 'Masoom' fetched RDB his second Filmfare Award as the 'Best Music Director' for its awesome scores. In case, you have still not figured out,* **Devi Dutt is the producer of 'Masoom,'** Shekhar Kapur's directorial debut. It may be recalled that, Panchamda was supposed to have kick-started his career as an independent composer with Guru Dutt's 'Raaz' (1957), but this movie was abruptly 'shelved.' The reclusive film-maker Devi Dutt shared information exclusively with the author **Chaitanya Padukone.** Excerpts from the interview:

Please share your memories with Panchamda during the mid-50's era.

Way back in 1956, I knew RDB well as a teenaged youngster when he accompanied my brother Guru Dutt, his singer-wife Geeta Dutt and me. We travelled in a spacious jeep for Sai Baba's darshan to Shirdi with the edited rushes of 'Pyaasa.' Even in those days, Pancham used to entertain us by playing wonderful extempore and Western tunes on his mouth-organ (harmonica) all through the journey. With an eye for discovering new talent, Guru Dutt-ji could spot the 'creative potential' of a 'budding music director' in Rahul. Much against the wishes of Rahul's dad, Sachin-da, Guru-ji even offered music direction assignments for his movies 'Raaz' and even 'Motu Ki Maasi' which not many people know. Unfortunately both films got shelved.

Enlighten us more about this little known project 'Mottu Ki Maasi.'

While 'Chaudhvin Ka Chand' was being shot, Guru Dutt suddenly decided to produce another comedy film 'Motu Ki Maasi' (remake of a Tamil film) and finalized my brother Atma Ram as director and R. D. Burman as the music director. We also recorded two songs written by Majrooh-saab and sung by Asha Bhonsle and Geeta Didi. This film cast comprised Salim Khan (Salman Khan's father), Tanuja, Johnny Walker and Mehmood. After seeing the rushes of the film shot for 'five days' Guru Dutt felt the film was lacking in comedy lines and he dropped the film giving no reasons to us. When my mother Vasanthi Padukone asked Guru Dutt the reason for stalling this film he just said, 'Don't worry, I will give Atma Ram another subject to direct.' This proved a major setback for R. D. Burman. But Guru Dutt compensated it when in 1961 Mehmood-bhaijaan approached him to give our entire crew and Guru Dutt Studios to shoot his first film, 'Chhote Nawab.' In fact Guru-ji was overjoyed to hear from Mehmood that he was giving a big break to R. D. Burman in this same film. The benevolent Guru Dutt also gifted two songs recorded for 'Motu Ki Maasi' to Panchamda.

Interestingly, in the rolling credit-titles of his next film 'Bhoot Bungla (1965),' Mehmood-bhaijaan has 'dedicated' the entire film to Guru Dutt, who had passed away by then.

It seems that RDB had 'first' played the harmonica for some other song-recording of Sachin-da's movie, much before 'Hai apna dil toh awara.'

Hmm, yes, it was in 1951, that I witnessed young boy Pancham brilliantly playing several mouth-organ pieces for the 'first time' in a recording for my brother Guru Dutt's 'Baazi.' It was for this film that Sachin-da composed the song 'Dil yeh kya cheez hai' sung by Kishore Kumar. It was picturized on Dev Anand playing the organ, against the backdrop of Khandala Ghats. Seven years later in '58, SDB made RDB play his mouth organ in the film 'Solva Saal' in which the lively song 'Hai apna dil toh awara' sung by Hemant-da was picturised on Dev-saab.

Wasn't it true that RDB drastically slashed his regular market price for the low budget film 'Masoom'?

That's right. Both director Shekhar Kapur and I had gone to first briefly meet Rahul. Since Guru Dutt-ji and I also had a close bonding with Pancham's parents (Sachin-da and Meera), his mother specifically told him that we should be treated like an 'extended' family. When she instructed him to give music in my film 'Masoom,' RDB did not say anything to her. Sometime later he told me that he would 'work for **free** as music director, but you must pay all the bills of the recording studio, singers and his team of musicians.' Instantly, I agreed but then as a gesture of appreciation, I voluntarily gave him a modest token amount of Rs.50,000/-, instead of his much higher market price.

There were whispers in music-biz, that RDB actually wanted Kishore Kumar to sing 'Tujhse naaraz'?

Quite true. RDB initially was keen that his close buddy Kishore Kumar should sing the haunting melody 'Tujh se naaraaz' which was the first recorded song for 'Masoom.' But since I had specially invited Kolkata-based Anup Ghoshal who was a National Award winning singer to Mumbai, I requested Pancham to allow Anup to at least record the song which Anup did so in the 'very first take.' Ultimately, Kishore-da, who was out of town, returned and heard Anup's song track, only to be delighted. The large-hearted Kishore-da was all praise for Ghoshal and prevailed upon Pancham to retain that track. An overjoyed Anup eventually 'refused' to charge any fees for that soul-stirring immortal melody.

Even for that National Award-winning heart-wrenching lullaby 'Do naina aur ek kahani' by Arati Mukherjee, there were rumours that an eminent playback singer was also there in the recording studio?

That way, Pancham was very frank and told me that he made Aarti sing because she has a good voice. Then came his disclaimer: 'however, if I do not like her song you must tell her in advance, that I may dub the track with Asha-ji's voice.' I looked at Gulzar-saab and Shekar and then came out to meet Aarti in her singer's cabin. I went to her and hinted her about the 'dubbing'—she smiled and said, 'I knew that this may happen after the recording; do not worry Devi-ji this happens in this industry. I will give you a great song.' The final recording started at around 12:30 pm and I could see RDB's face smiling and nodding at Gulzar and sound recordist Kaushik-saab and everyone heard the recorded track. Meanwhile Aarti hurriedly took her payment and discreetly left without meeting anyone. Nobody was praising the song because apparently Asha-didi had arrived. She too was listening to the recorded track in the recording room with Kaushik, Pancham, Gulzar and Shekar Kapur. I was very sure that Asha didi may not approve the song and I was expecting a blast from her, but when I entered with my wife Chanda in the recording room Asha-didi graciously told me in Marathi, 'You have been creating good singers. This song by Aarti is just superb and it cannot be dubbed by me or by anyone else. It was another feather on my cap. These magnanimous gestures by such legendary singers like Kishore-da, Asha-didi and later even Lata-didi (who sang the female version of 'Tujhe Naaraaz') were only because they respected my bhabhi, singer Geeta Dutt, as well as Guru Dutt, who were both essentially good human beings.'

Reminisces Devi Dutt, 'At the 'Lakdi ki kaatthi' music-sitting, within no time, the multi-faceted genius Gulzar-saab fluently 'hummed' a 'bachcha limerick song', often recited by kids in Old Delhi, that too with the same basic local ethnic tune. He wrote the lyrics within 30 minutes and suggested a basic tune format to Pancham. An amazed RDB stared at him and said, "*Kya baat hai Gulzar-saab, aap gaane ke saath, mujhe tune bhi de rahe hain.*" Then RDB took over, to improvise the song-tune, add his original flavor, finesse and finishing touches. The final foot-tapping song turned out to be an all-time favourite with kids. It also proves that Pancham too had a 'naughty child' within him. Call it a divine coincidence that Jugal Hansraj's moppet-kid screen-character was named 'Rahul'!

COMPOSER ANANDJI SHAH

VETERAN BOLLYWOOD COMPOSER OF LEGENDARY
DUO 'KALYANJI-ANANDJI'

'Music was Pancham's religion and he was fully devoted to it. There has been speculative data floating on the Internet that RDB played 'harmonica' for one of our songs, which is false and baseless. During the golden era of the 60s and 70s, when he met us or vice versa, he would be carrying his 'mouth-organ,' like how we now carry a cell-phone. So it was 'wrongly' presumed that he played for our recordings. Kalyanji-bhai and I shared a closed bonding with his dad maestro Sachin-da and also with Rahul. Both RDB and us (Kalyanji and Anadji) regularly recorded at Film Center in different shifts or on different days. Often we would attend his recordings and at times he would come and watch our 'takes.' There was no tension, no envy and no insecurity those days—it was mutual harmony. There used to be lot of masti-mazaak between us and RDB loved to relish Gujarati snacks after adding spice to it. By nature he was such a helpful soul that he even went out of his way, at times. We had this 'live' Kalyanji-Anandji Musical Show, I think it was probably for the customs authorities, in Bombay (Mumbai). At the eleventh hour, for personal reasons, Kishore Kumar backed out and only Asha Bhosle turned up for the concert. Now when Pancham came to know, he himself called us up and said he was willing to come and perform. And the show was a smash hit, because Pancham was 'singing' with Asha-ji while Kalyanji and I were conducting the orchestra on stage. It was a 'unique' manoranjan for the audience. As regard his ability to adapt Western tunes, I consider RDB an 'intercontinental' composer. Because whether it was a Japanese melody or an Arabic gypsy *dhun* or Latin American jazz or even African wild rhythm he would skillfully blend their flavour into his songs. There is no harm in being occasionally inspired, as long as at least 80 percent is original. When it came to classical numbers he was in total command. Gulzar-saab, I feel, has extracted RDB's best raga-based scores. Content with his work, Pancham was too laid-back to generate media-hype for himself, which was his drawback. Geniuses are not created, they are 'born.' That explains how creating immortal music was his 'birthright."

"The music and showbiz professional impact of RDB's music continues to enchant an awe-struck generation of music aficionados and connoisseurs alike"—Sanjeev (Madan Mohan) Kohli— senior music-biz 'n' showbiz professional.

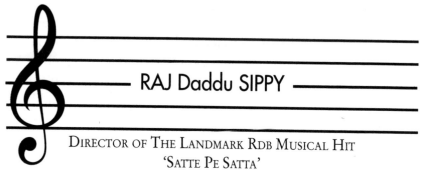

RAJ Daddu SIPPY

DIRECTOR OF THE LANDMARK RDB MUSICAL HIT
'SATTE PE SATTA'

Pataa nahin why, but initially I was not at all impressed with the title-song 'Dukki pe dukki ho.' But Punch (RDB) confidently said, 'Trust me this song will be a chartbuster—you wait and watch.' I blindly trusted him and ultimately music-history proved me wrong.'

'While the rest of the music-biz and his fans referred to him as 'Pancham-da' or RDB, I guess I was the only one who called him 'Punch,' and he lived up to his name in all his memorable songs. That is to say, he would thrust his solid musical punches and stun his rivals and impress his listeners. Call it uncanny coincidence that he also composed music for my directorial movie titled 'Boxer'!

My relationship with RDB goes back to the late '60s and early '70s era, when landmark comedy musicals like 'Padosan' and 'Bombay to Goa' with his brilliant scores, were produced by my dad (N. C. Sippy). The Punch *parampara* continued when my producer-brother Romu Sippy launched 'Satte Pe Satta (SPS)' which I directed. And with its Indianised innovative 'world music' scores, it turned out to be a benchmark trendsetter for all times to come. What I loved about RDB was that he was a candidly honest and yet a caring composer who wanted to give his best output to his film-makers in every possible way. Pataa nahin why, but initially I had almost rejected the title-song

'Dukki pe dukki ho.' But Punch (RDB) confidently said, 'Trust me, this song will be a chartbuster—you wait and watch.' I blindly trusted him and ultimately music-history proved me wrong.

Besides his sound knowledge of sound-balancing and mixing, Punch possessed the hidden genes of a 'director' as well. That's because he would spontaneously suggest visuals and props for my songs, like he suggested that we should have Sachin playing the harmonica (mouth-organ) in 'Satte Pe Satta.'

The gradually increasing tempo of 'Pyaar hamein kis mod pe' in Satte Pe Satta is perhaps a unique song with multiple singers. During the song recordings, Pancham used to sing with the singers on one mic and used to tip-toe across to the other mic to play his harmonica and get back again to his original position. That then was his zestful enthusiasm. **Even that song 'Jhuka ke sar ko' from 'SPS' was his brainchild.**

Deviating from Western music he even came up with a haunting semi-classical number 'Roz roz aankhon taley' from Jeeva. The entire credit for this melody track goes to Pancham and Gulzar-saab. Not just songs and interludes, RDB was equally innovative at coming up with on the spot bizarre concepts for background music scores. Like the way he made singer Annette Pinto resort to 'gargling' water to create a scary visual for Amitabh Bachchan's exit from jail in 'SPS' and for Danny Denzongpa's entry in 'Andar Baahar.' This same gargle effect was used in 'Sitamgar' and also for Dharmendra in 'Qayamat.'

Basically Punch was a 'fun-atic'—he loved to indulge in masti, as he enjoyed his non-vegetarian food, his drinks, his pranks and his smoke sessions. Nothing could stop him. At the 'Film Center' there used to be prominent sign-board which screamed 'Lungs at Work-No Smoking.' But being a rebel, he used to sit below that board and light his cigarette and then it would be my turn. Only the two of us were allowed to fag-drag out there. **On a personal level, Pancham-da was very fond of using abusive slang (read 'gaalis') with his close friends. Not that he meant to hurt or humiliate, but it was part**

of his persona. Ironically, if he did not use it, I would gently ask him—'Punch' are you okay today?

Some months before he departed from this world, RDB met me at some event. There he made an uncanny statement which rattled me and gives me goosebumps even today. *"Jaane se pehley, main keela (nail) thokh kar jaaonga!"* Oh my God! What a platinum 'keela' he has hammered on the wall of eternal fame.

On 4 January, during the wee hours when Punch passed away, I reached his house within ten minutes as I stayed in the same area. But I did not go up to his apartment to see him in that lifeless state. Instead I stood below his building and paid my homage, because it was sheer disbelief that I could not reconcile to the shocking reality that RDB was no more, but I was there right up to the time until the funeral cortege started. Am sure he is up there, creating lovely, lively music for all the blessed souls and divine forces in heaven.'

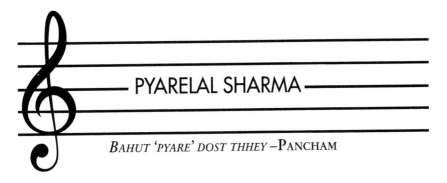

PYARELAL SHARMA

BAHUT 'PYARE' DOST THHEY –PANCHAM

"Woh jab yaad aaye, bahut yaad aaye."

Legendary Bollywood maestro composer Pyarelal pays tribute to Panchamda (R. D. Burman).

Waltzing into a nostalgic flashback, Pyarelal (of the legendary **Laxmikant-Pyarelal duo**) vividly recounts how his 'late' partner Laxmikant and he were associated as musicians and arrangers with sangeetkaar RDB's initial movies 'Chhote Nawaab' and 'Bhoot Bangla' in the early 60s which had some outstanding music.

We had a great time in those days jamming music and indulging in bouts of *masti-mazaak* because we were in our twenties sailing in the same rocking boat. And fun-loving prankster Pancham who was well-trained, proved his classical music forte with his masterpiece 'Ghar aaja ghir aaye' but also dabbled merrily with rock 'n' roll when he came up with 'Aao twist karen.' Right from the beginning Rahul aspired to be a different yet versatile music composer and wanted to break free from being overshadowed by his father Sachin Dev Burman. He had inherited the musical genes from his dad Sachin-da who is again a legend with his own classy repertoire.

Why RD was asked to play harmonica for L.P. in 'Dosti' songs?

Way back in 1964, when Laxmi-ji and I were composing for 'Dosti,' we had a harmonica theme in the songs especially 'Raahi manwa dukhki chinta.' So we instantly approached our buddy Burman, because he was a 'passionate' harmonica player. Although RDB was also recording for a song on that day in some other studio, he managed to attend our recording and played so beautifully. So that was the *"dosti ka tohfaa"* which Pancham gave us.

What made the super-talented RDB 'undermine' some of his best composed music?

Apparently, the futuristic composer was disillusioned earlier when his masterpiece music in milestone movies like 'Teesri Manzil,' 'Amar Prem,' 'Padosan,' 'Jawani Diwani,' 'Kati Patang' and 'Hare Rama Hare Krishna' were 'not' given due formal recognition by way of prestigious awards. Like when he won his second Filmfare Award for 'Masoom' I lavishly complimented him. Strangely, he did not seem very thrilled about the recognition and casually brushed it off, as his mediocre effort.

Pyare-bhai, which are your all-time favourite RDB music tracks?

'Aap Ki Kasam,' 'Amar Prem,' and of course 'Padosan.' Believe me I am simply addicted to 'Padosan,' I must have watched this rom-com movie dozens of times, but I still love to watch it again, because of its out-of-the world music which ranges from the Western 'Main chali main chali' to the whacko comic take on classical music 'Ek chatur naar.' In fact, it's my open friendly challenge to any contemporary composer to come up with equally amazing music tracks like those in 'Padosan.'

Isn't it true that you get 'irritated' listening to the grunting bass rasp vocals (as in the antara in 'Duniya mein' from Apna Desh)?

That's right. This grating vocals style which was practiced by certain singers abroad, somehow had never appealed to me. When my partner Laxmi-ji tried to use those grunting vocals in one of our movies, I asked him to delete those portions from the audio track. But this is strictly my personal opinion on using bizarre sounds in vocals. All the same, I highly appreciate Pancham's experimental guts at being successfully different.

What according to you was Pancham's forte, while composing songs? What about his flair for lifting foreign tunes?

Always having a sharp focus on the subject and theme of his movies was RDB's forte. For instance, he composed only college youth-centric songs for 'Jawani Diwani' and 'Khel Khel Mein.' In 'Hare Rama Hare Krishna' in three of the hit songs including 'Dum maro dum,' he has blended chorus chanting of 'Hare Krishna' mantra using different tunes. Internationally, one is allowed to lift upto four bars or sixteen beats. But if it goes beyond sixteen beats it would attract copyright laws. Even when Pancham sometimes adapted from foreign tracks or from regional folk it was mostly an 'essence inspiration' of the initial bars and notes. The rest of the songs generally had his own distinct RDB signature melody and orchestration. Even Laxmi-ji and I were inspired by a catchy Lebanese folk-tune, the essence of which we used in our hit dance song mukhda 'Jaagi badan mein jwala' in 'Izzat'.

Any last thoughts on the untimely demise of the brilliant composer-singer?

During the 60s, Pancham would often race ahead in his own car and would go out-of-sight while we were slowly trailing behind in our car. Looks like he did it again in January '94; only this time he was not waiting for us five junctions ahead with his naughty expression, but vanished hamesha ke liye, into the blues of eternity. Maestros like R. D. Burman are born perhaps once in a millennium. With his legacy of popular evergreen hit songs still being played regularly and even recycled so often, he will always remain the most dazzling star in the musical sky. *Woh jab yaad aaye, bahut yaad aaye.*

Bade dilwala! When I asked Pancham-da as to why 'rival' Laxmikant played the role of a music director in a hit song from 'Teri Kasam' for which RD had scored fabulous songs, he replied, 'It so happened that Laxmi happens to be a 'good friend' of the producer of that film and they were shooting those portions in a studio near his bungalow, so they roped him in. May I mention here that Laxmi is a very close friend of mine right from the days when we both were 'unemployed.' We both learnt to booze together. But today, with these hectic schedules, we rarely meet. In those days we even composed together.'—Panchamda

HEMA MALINI

SENIOR BOLLYWOOD ACTRESS, M.P. &
EMINENT CLASSICAL DANSEUSE

'There is this popular misconception that R. D. Burman specializes mainly in Western songs, because most of his popular 'remixes' are Western numbers. Frankly speaking there is no need to remix his songs because *vaise bhi* the original RDB songs sound as if they have been composed and recorded just recently. Such was his futuristic forte for orchestration. As an actress I consider myself very fortunate that I have acted in around eighteen films with RDB's music. **Since I am a trained classical danseuse, I wish to emphasise that for me, Panchamda's classical music caliber was par excellence. If you watch and hear RDB's masterpiece songs in my movies like 'Khushboo,' 'Kinaara,' 'Mehbooba' and of course 'Kudrat,' you will know what I mean. Among my favorites is 'Naam gum jaayega,' 'Meethe bol bole,' 'Ek hi khwaab kaee,' 'Toone O rangeelay' and of course 'Humey tum se pyar.'** Even in a spectacular action-thriller dacoit-drama like 'Sholay,' Panchamda came up with such tantalizing taal-tarang percussion in the song 'Jab tak hai jaan.' Despite the shards of broken glass that were strewn around, I was engrossed in dancing to the captivating dhun and beats of that RDB song. Among the other RDB music-centric films of mine, 'Seeta Aur Geeta,' 'Paraya Dhan' and 'Joshilaa' have such marvelous variety of songs. At premieres or film events, **the unassuming Pancham-da would coyly come up to** me and say, "*Humne aapke liye bahut achhe gaane banaaye hain,* hope you will like them."

'As an actress, I am only an 'instrument' in the hands of the director and music director. The credit also goes to the entire crew and my co-stars because after all, it's a concerted team effort. **Ek khaas attribute I have observed about Panchamda, is that he knew precisely how to attract and enthrall the masses with his catchy music.** One of my earlier movies 'Waaris' (1969) was known for the racy 'Ek bechara thaa' and the other 'Lehara ke aaya hai' which had a scintillating Arabic flavor. Both these songs had a terrific 'repeat value.' In film music-biz, **RDB is proclaimed by so many as the 'numero uno,' for his trend-setting deluge of talent that still continues to 'make waves' and I fully endorse that.'**

"Pancham and I were good buddies. The very fact that I named my son 'Rahul 'after him, one can realize the high esteem I had for him. Initially I used to play the tabla, but soon I switched over to the santoor. It was RDB who compelled me to revive my taal-talent and made me play tabla for the song recording-take of this classical song 'Saiyaan Beimaan' from the film 'Guide' (1965) which had his father Sachin-da's score. During our drives in his car I observed that RDB was highly rhythm-centric by nature." —**Pandit Shivkumar Sharma**—acclaimed santoor maestro & film composer.

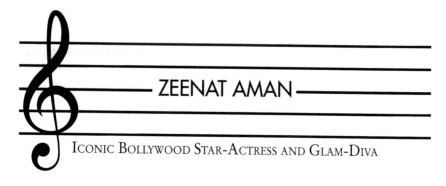

ZEENAT AMAN

Iconic Bollywood Star-Actress and Glam-Diva

'The musical revolutionary who dared to rebel against conventional norms and come up with **'refreshingly different'** Western and raga-based gems—**that's R. D. Burman for me and all his ardent fans.** Without being apprehensive of rejection, legendary Panchamda had the genius to infuse infectious brilliance in his chartbuster songs, which then hugely connected with the masses. It was as if, **he was living up to that lyrical line** *'Hum sub ki parwaa karen kyon,'* **from my iconic immortal haunting hippie anthem** 'Dum maro dum' which he specially created for my screen-character 'Janice.' Whether it is 'Hum dono do premi' or 'Samundar mein nahaake' or 'Chura liya hai tumne' or even 'Pyar mein dil ki maar di goli'; **each RDB song picturised on me, is a unique jewel that sparkles in my career crown.** It's my honour and privilege that **as the leading lady I have the highest number of Hindi movies (twenty-five)** whose music is scored by the modest maestro fondly hailed by his team of ace musicians as 'R D Boss'! Indeed, he will eternally reign as the 'Boss of retro film music!'

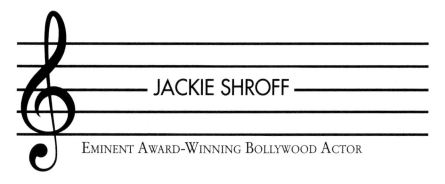

JACKIE SHROFF

EMINENT AWARD-WINNING BOLLYWOOD ACTOR

This rendezvous of mine with the affable Jackie Shroff took place within the campus of Subhash Ghai's Whistling Woods Institute (WWI) campus at Film City. It was also a late night birthday celebration of Ghai convened by all his WWI students and alumni. As usual, the suave style-icon Shroff stood in a secluded corner and as I went across to greet him, I overheard him singing the RDB number 'Jab andhera hota hai.' That was the emotional-trigger point for Jaggu-dada to glide into a flashback mode and 'recall Rahul Dev.' Over to Jackie:

'Not many people know that I signed on Vidhu Vinod Chopra's 'Parinda' after I became *fidaa* over that waltz number 'Tumse milkar aisa lagaa,' which my co-star Anil Kapoor made me listen to, in his car. Moreover, Anil even told me that this classy R. D. Burman song was to be picturised on him and not on me. Yet, without even hearing the detailed initial narration, I started shooting for that awesome movie. A year later, I bagged the coveted Filmfare Award for the 'Best Actor' for my role in 'Parinda.' All thanks to Pancham-da for being instrumental and inspiring me to go ahead.'

'Bhidu, right from my childhood days when I was residing at Teen Batti area (Mumbai), I used to adore the song 'Ghar aaja ghir aaye.' Then the music of 'Bhoot Bungla'—I also loved RDB as a comedian on-screen, followed by the terrific 'Teesri Manzil' numbers as I was an ardent fan of Shammi Kapoor too. A string of chartbuster albums like 'Padosan,' 'Jawani Diwani,' 'Namak Haram,' 'Aap Ki Kasam' are among my top favourites, but the list is endless. Many years later, when I had turned into a 'hippie' the trance music of 'Hare Rama Hare Krishna' used to freak me out. **Ufff, that 'wah-wah' sound after that 'hushsh' and that guitar strumming of 'Dum maro dum' was itself a musical nashaa for me. At the same time, I used to have my eyes welled with tears whenever I heard that sentimental song 'Phoolon ka taaron ka.' Even now emotionally,** *meri vaatt lag jaati hai,* **when I hear that track. Maybe because in real life, I don't have a 'sister.'** *Hazaar salaam* **Pancham-da, for all those musical gems.'**

'Guess it was a God-sent memorable opportunity that I was the anchor-host of this '1942: A LoveStory' film completion event where I had to call Panchamda on the stage. The songs in '1942: A Love Story' directed by Vidhu Vinod Chopra are so divine—in that genre like *sufiyana.* Listen carefully to the lyrics and the beautiful rhythmic melody of 'Ek ladki ko dekha' and you will know what I mean. Even the haunting song which goes 'Yeh safar bahut kathin hai magar' and has this initial fleeting glimpse of legendary Sachin-da's 'Pyaasa' song 'Jaane woh kaise' is like a devotional bhajan—I feel I am so lucky that one of Panchamda's soulful melodies composed by him just before he left us all, is picturised on me. **Once again, thanks to Panchamda's blessings I won the Filmfare Award for 'Best Supporting Actor' even for '1942: A Love Story.'** Whenever I met RDB at parties or at recordings, I shared such warm *'apnapan' with him. It's difficult to explain, but I have a soulful bonding with Panchamda.* **When he suddenly passed away, I was intensely shocked and shattered at his funeral—he was 'family' to me. Although I miss him, he always lives in my heart, having grown up on the addiction called R. D. 'Bur-mania'!'**

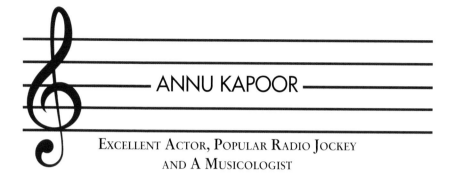

ANNU KAPOOR

EXCELLENT ACTOR, POPULAR RADIO JOCKEY AND A MUSICOLOGIST

'R. D. Burman is the most remembered and influential music director among the present lot of music lovers, singers and music directors. He introduced Western electronics and experimented with sound craft. The same as what Rehman is doing today but the Melody remained intact in RDB's compositions most of the time and he was fortunate to have Majrooh and Anand Bakshi as lyricists to present a memorable song.'

Annu's favorite five RDB songs

1. Ghar aaja ghir aaye (Chote Nawab/Shailendra)
2. Kya janu sajan hoti hai kya (Baharon Ke Sapne/Majrooh)
3. Tumne mujhe dekha (Teesri Manzil/Majrooh)
4. Na ja O mere humdum (Pyar Ka Mausam/Majrooh)
5. Kehna hai kehna hai (Padosan/Rajendra Krishan)

SHAILENDRA SINGH

NOTED PLAYBACK SINGER

AAJ SHAAM KO 'JAMMTE' HAIN, WOULD BE THE SANGEETKAAR'S FAVORITE CATCH-PHRASE.

Pancham-da said 'cheers' as rain-water poured into our glasses: recalls noted senior playback singer-actor Shailendra Singh revealing the celebrated composer's fun-loving flip-side.

'In recognition of his phenomenal contribution to Bollywood retro music, legendary composer-singer R. D. Burman should be posthumously conferred with the prestigious Dadasaheb Phalke

National Award or maybe the Padma Bhushan. Ideally, some prominent music training academy should also be named after him,' insists senior singer-actor Shailendra Singh, who was among the very few loyal close buddies of Panchamda who always stood by him, even during the sangeetkaar's depressing, almost jobless, slump career phase.

Jogging into memory-lane, Shailendra, who has sung a string of evergreen RDB chartbusters such as 'Humne tumko dekha' in 'Khel Khel Mein' and 'Hoga tumse pyara kaun' in Zamane Ko Dikhana Hain, 'Jaane do naa' in Saagar, feels that Pancham's forte was his futuristic foresight to know what precisely would click with the audiences, 'which is why he could boldly experiment with weird sound effects and while singing, using rasp, grunt bass vocals as in the chartbuster song 'Duniya mein' in 'Apna Desh.' Recalls Shailendra, who was given his singing debut-break in 'Bobby' by showman Raj Kapoor, 'very few are aware, that when I gave my first voice 'audition' for 'Bobby' in the presence of composer Laxmikant-ji, I sang the RDB composition 'Dekha naa haaye re' in 'Bombay to Goa' and Rajesh 'Raju' Roshan was playing the conga drums. After hearing me out, Laxmi-ji smiled and conveyed his approval.

At the star-studded muhurat of 'Bobby,' it was Panchamda who clamoured for my formal introduction on stage. That's how he connected with me. Impressed with my vocal talent, he later got me on board to sing in 'Khel Khel Mein,' which also had the legendary Kishore-da's tracks,' reveals Singh who has sung a peppy playback duet number with 'diva' actress Rekha! The song is 'Kal toh Sunday ki chutti hai' in Agar Tum Na Hote. Since I had also acted as the hero opposite Rekha in the movie 'Agreement,' I shared good rapport with her. But full credit goes to the versatile melody-king Panchamda for discovering Rekha's singing potential,' shrugs the trained actor-singer who feels that RDB had a 'soft corner' for singers if they were not fine-tuned for the song-recording. 'It happened once when I was unable to sing with my full-throated voice-throw. The moment RDB realized that he announced 'pack-up' and said, 'let's record your song after maybe two-three days, once your voice gets perfect'.' According to 'Shailu' (that's what the composer fondly called him) his bonding with 'fun-loving prankster RDB' was very special. 'We often went for long-drives with music playing on RDB's very expensive car stereo system and we also had joint booze sessions. *Aaj shaam ko jammte hain,*' would be the sangeetkaar's favorite catch-phrase. Way back in 1981, I was driving my car, returning home from Cuffe Parade (South Mumbai), after the song-recording of the title song 'Zamaane ko dikhaana hai.' The exuberant Pancham-da and I started drinking and legendary Nasir Hussain-saab was also sitting in my car. Just imagine two iconic showbiz luminaries with me—those were eternally euphoric moments. Those days, apparently there were no explicit restrictions on consuming liquor when driving. When we reached Linking Road at Bandra, the roads were flooded. As I had anticipated, my car got stalled. It was around midnight and still pouring heavily outside. Suddenly we realized that the soda-water was over. Not surprisingly, RDB had this idea in his head and quipped 'thrust your glass out and blend it with pure rain-water and let's say cheers.'

That then was Pancham in his 'true colours," smiles Shailendra who still recounts his 'last' live concert with RDB around Christmas time in **Cochin (Kochi), Kerala.** 'The show was a 'sell-out' and the local Southside music-savvy audience went bonkers over all the RDB Hindi chartbuster songs. Some of them later came backstage and cajoled RDB that during 1994, he would try to compose songs for **at least 'one' Malayalam film.** They were aware that he had already given popular music earlier for Tamil and Telugu movies. But their ardent wish remained 'unfulfilled' as he abruptly exited this world leaving his legion of fans in a state of shock.'

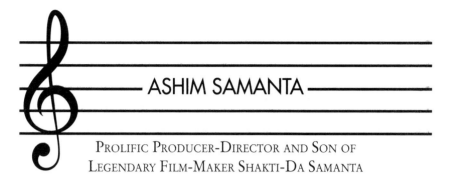

ASHIM SAMANTA

PROLIFIC PRODUCER-DIRECTOR AND SON OF
LEGENDARY FILM-MAKER SHAKTI-DA SAMANTA

"With his vision for visuals Pancham-da could have possibly 'directed' a movie as well": Ashim Samanta

"Like the kid in 'Amar Prem,' RDB too was 'badaa natkhat' at heart. At my wedding ceremony he kept on whispering in my ear, "it's not too late—you may still back out from the alliance—don't give up your independence" etc etc," recalls Ashim Samanta

It remains a 'unique' composition till date

"For my dad Shakti-da and me, R D Burman was our family member first and then a film music composer. A compassionate fun-loving and a good-food loving human being whose only passion was being drowned in music. I had met Pancham-da during the Kati Patang and Amar Prem days. The gap between father, Pancham and me was nearly 15 years years on either side. He was elder brother to me and younger brother to my father. My first connectivity with RDB was during the 'Amar Prem ' and 'Kati Patang' days both at home and at song-recordings as well. The way Pancham made such an effortless shift in that vibrant song 'Aaj na chhodenge….khelenge hum holi' (Kati Patang) proved his calibre to swiftly oscillate between fast-tempo mukhdaa with Kishoreda's vocal antics to the relatively slow-paced Lata-didi's raga-based antara. It left me wonder-struck. The other cabaret song 'Mera Naam Hai Shabnam.' The composition is so 'unique' that even if I hear it today, I feel the same thrill with the pulsating rhythm playing, even as Asha Bhosle is rap-reciting sensuously in the 'monologue' format. Simply mind-blowing!

Background scores ka baadshah...

Besides being a competent composer he was a music director—let me stress on the word 'director'. Because not only with Dad and me, even with other eminent film-makers he would spontaneously suggest 'scenes' and 'visuals' to go with the music of the songs. The masses relate to Panchamda mostly because of his chartbusting songs. But I would insist he was also a maestro of 'background music'. Even his rolling credits title-music of most of his films blended with the subject of his movies, that he was giving music for. Besides giving visual suggestions, for my movie 'Palay Khan' starring Jackie Shroff, he specially arranged for an Afghani musical instrument with sharp sounds. Which has been played in the background as well as for the songs 'Salma Ko Mil Gaya' and 'Allah Kare' and 'Kaabul Se Aaya.' The witty Pancham would often say 'background score is like our heartbeats, it brings the scene to 'life.' Because if you mute the music, the scene becomes almost 'lifeless.' That's because our 'hearing' senses are much more sensitive and receptive.

In 'Amar Prem' when Sharmila Tagore sees her ex-husband die, the milk in the vessel is shown boiling, as she goes into a flash-back mode. I remember, that RDB recorded a back-ground music piece but played it in 'reverse' to suit the scene. It sounded weird at first, but when you watch the movie you realize the 'method in his madness.' Sometimes, 'RD can also stand for 'reverse direction' he had quipped." Yet another compelling score was the 'Aradhana' haunting back-ground music piece when 'beta' Rajesh Khanna is introduced to aged mother Sharmila Tagore. It gives you the goose bumps and moves you to tears. Hats off to Pancham for his awesome conception—after all he was the 'associate music director.' In my own movie 'Aamne Saamne' which I directed, there was this 'slow motion' action sequence between Sanjay Dutt and Shakti Kapoor. With his ingenious foresight-vision RD was adamant that we should record a 'fast tempo' rhythmic musical piece.

When I heard his suggestion I found it very odd. But he had his logic in place. 'Agar fight scene slow hai to shaayad boring bhi ho sakta hai. But fast beats would bring the jolted audience to the edge of their seats,' he justified. Although I was not too sure I said okay, lets go for it. And when I saw the final scene merged with the background track, I exclaimed "Dada You are a super genius! With his vision for visuals Pancham-da could have possibly 'directed' a movie as well"

Pancham had this amazing 'sporting spirit'...

Over the decades there has been avid speculation that at the insistence of Kaka-ji (Rajesh Khanna) my dad Shakti-da had preferred to switch over to Laxmikant Pyarelal for 'Anurodh' (1977). The grapevine insists that the temperamental Khanna apparently had a nasty tiff with (his close buddy) Panchamda and consequently prevailed upon Shakti-da to deviate from his favourite composer. To the best of my knowledge, these rumours are a figment of wild imagination. Not many people know, that my dad (Shakti-da) was a close friend of Laxmikant-jee and used to attend his private birthday parties which mostly coincided during Diwali festivities. During one of those occasions, Laxmi-jee kept coaxing my Dad—'Shakti-da hamare saath ek toh film karo.' That was when Dad decided to work with L.P. and simultaneously working with Pancham-da in three different films including 'Mehbooba' (with Rajesh Khanna) and 'The Great Gambler' and 'Balika Badhu.' For that matter, for 'Amaanush,' my dad had signed on Shyamal Mitra as the composer.

Very few people know that when I made this movie 'Aakhri Baazi' (1989) instead of working with RDB, I took an impulsive decision and signed on Anu Malik. That's because Anu had come to meet me in my office. After listening to a couple of 'situations,' Anu instantly composed two songs that too with the lyrics and he floored me outright. So much so that I paid him a token 'signing amount.' When Dad heard about my decision, he was so peeved and he stormed 'are you mad.' But then, I made Anu come for an 'encore' and play his tunes again in the presence of my dad after which he was pacified and he relented.

Now my 'kashmakash' was— 'how to face Panchamda'? As all this had happened without his knowledge. Days later, when RDB came to meet me, he seemed to already 'know' what had transpired. Guess, my dad must have confided in him. Pancham could sense the awkwardness I was going thru and he could read my uneasy facial expressions. Which is when I disclosed it's just for one film that Anu's scoring the music.' I was mentally prepared for a nasty repartee from Pancham. But he was made of sterner stuff and could withstand turbulent weather, is what I later realized. Can you believe it, he was so 'sporting' that he 'gracefully' complimented me for my conviction. Hush, I heaved a sigh of relief.

Bada natkhat hai rey...

Like the little kid in 'Amar Prem' RDB too was 'badaa natkhat at heart.' At my wedding ceremony he constantly kept on whispering in my ear, "it's not too late—you may still back out from the alliance—abhi bhi soch ley—don't give up your independence" etc etc,. My wife being a Gujarati couldn't figure out RDB's Bengali commentary. After 'pack-up' Pancham was altogether a different person. Whenever he came for my Dad's birthday parties he would be the 'jaan' and 'shaan' of the party with his witty lively nature, his 'non-veg' jokes, his witty jibes and the bonhomie aura. They all loved him and respected him as well.

All those who surmise that this classical song 'Bada Natkhat Hai' of 'Amar Prem' was 'improvised' by Sachin-da Burman, should cross-check with me before making such statements. The song was composed by RDB and finalized by my Dad Shakti-da in my presence. In fact I was in my bedroom when I faintly heard Pancham singing the semi-devotional track 'Bada Natkhat Hai Rey' as he played on his harmonium. Honestly, I was so fascinated that a little later I rushed out and requested him to play it all over again. It was late evening, I remember, and RDB said 'not now Ashim, its time for sips of booze.' But then Dad also requested him, so he had to comply and we heard it again. The track sung by RD sounds divine, although the final take was in Lata-didi's mesmerizing voice.

POORNIMA - SUSHMA SHRESTHA

ACCOMPLISHED POPULAR PLAYBACK SINGER

'It's by divine intervention that the hit song 'Tera mujhse hai pehle ka naata koi' which I sang for RDB actually symbolizes my instant close rapport and family relationship with the great composer-singer. For me throughout his life, Pancham-da was always like a protective elder brother. Originally, RDB wanted an established leading singer to sing this song for the musical hit movie, 'Aa Gale Lag Ja.' So I was called by Dada to record the duet song with Kishore-da, with the explicit understanding that my track would be 'dubbed' later on by a top singer. But as destiny willed, the legendary director Manmohan 'Manji' Desai heard my track and was apparently very impressed. So much so, that he recommended to RDB that he should 'retain' my voice and need not get it dubbed. Can you believe, more than me, it was RDB who was overjoyed? The genius rushed to the singer's booth to share this *"khush khabri."* 'The song is yours,' he exclaimed, as I turned euphoric.

Since my father, noted music-composer, Bhola Shreshtha used to be a close friend of the Maestro Sachin Dev Burman, I used to get special attention and even partial treatment from Rahul-da. **As a child-artiste singer I sang RDB's superhit compositions like the 'Yaadon ki baarat' title-song and also 'Saare ke saare in Parichay.' Even when we were in a chorus-group, Dada used to make me stand, right in the front to lead the group.**

Some years later, I felt so privileged when I was called to record the evergreen soulful song 'Kya hua tera vaada' with iconic Mohammed Rafi-saab. There was some extra-special vibes about that song which I felt while recording. And I was so thrilled when eventually Rafi-saab won the coveted National Award as well as the Filmfare Award for that same track.

One of my most memorable moments was 'sharing' the recording mic with Pancham-da during the song 'Bade achhe lagte hain' in Balika Badhu where in the interlude Dada sings, 'O-O-O maajhi rey...' In Amit Kumar's lilting solo, I just sing that one-word 'aur,' in every mukhdaa. For me singing for RDB—even just that much meant such an honour for me. Yet another golden opportunity was getting to sing the fabulous number 'Ek din bik jaayega' in Dharam Karam with the revered legend Mukesh-ji. At the song-recording it was also my privileged honour to be interacting with luminaries like 'showman' Raj Kapoor-saab, director Randhir Kapoor-sir, Sachin-da and of course composer R. D. Burman. Both Raj-ji and Pancham-da were so gentle and encouraging and highly appreciated my 'perfect singing' especially that musical phrase *"Ta rum pum."* Honestly, RDB went out of his way to ensure that I should be part of this landmark R.K. banner song—I can never ever forget his supreme kind-hearted gesture. As a music guru, I learnt from him the correct vocal mic techniques of how to laugh and cry naturally, the falsetto and how to bring out guttural (throat) sounds.

Not just recordings, I used to also accompany Pancham-da quite often on his 'live' overseas concerts where I would sing on stage with him, chartbuster songs like 'Piya tu ab toh aaja.' **There was a time, when I was badly in need of funds, a few lakhs, for buying my first house in Mumbai.** So hesitatingly I conveyed it to RDB through his manager Bharat Ashar. The next time I went to meet Dada at his apartment, he seemed to already know what my problem was. Calling me inside his room he opened his cupboard safe and told me, 'take as much as you want.' Even as I made attempts to tell him, that he should adjust the payments against my overseas shows remuneration, he refused to listen and gestured me to leave with the money. **What does one call such a benevolent human being, Rahul 'Dev,' yes he was also a 'God' sent Samaritan.**

During 1992–93, whenever I would visit RDB he would be delighted and say *"mera bachcha ghar aa gaya."* With hardly any work on hand, Dada seemed to be quite disturbed and lonely, seeking solace in the company of anyone who would visit him. On 4 January 1994, early morning I was told that Dada was very unwell. **When I rushed to his Marylands apartment and saw him lying 'lifeless,' I was totally speechless, devastated and on the verge of collapse.** In fact Gulzar-saab who was in the same room looked at me and said to the others, 'please take care of her.' **The mentor whom I had idolized all my life, would never ever say again** *"mera bachcha ghar aa gaya."*

'PADMA BHUSHAN' UDIT NARAYAN JHA–

TALENTED SENIOR PLAYBACK SINGER

RDB kehte hain, bada naam karega

"*Tumhari jackpot lottery nikalne wali hai*", Panchamda said confidently after hearing my audio-tracks at the 'Qayamat Sey Qayamat Tak (QSQT)' (1988) music release party. "*Tumhari anokhi aawaz screen-par Aamir Khan se bilkul match karti hai, kya baat hai.*" I can never forget Panchamda's morale-boosting prophecy which made my day and all the days ever after, because I never looked back after that. Having acquired name, fame and success, honestly speaking, at that release event, 'showman' Nasir Hussain-saab's best wishes and RDB's blessings meant 'the world' to me. As is known to all my fans, I eventually won the Filmfare Best Male Playback Award for the 'QSQT' song 'Papa kehte hain.'

I think I must have sung around five RDB compositions out of which the waltzy duet song 'Jeevan ke din chhote sahee' in 'Bade Dil Wala'(1983) with Lata-Didi, is very popular. Prior to the big-break that I got with 'QSQT,' I would often visit Panchamda in his sitting room or at his recordings. Every time, Dada would cheer me and say 'I am eagerly waiting for that day, when I can use your vibrant voice for a newly-launched hero for 'all' the songs in the movie.' But then destiny had other alternate plans for me. My favorite RDB albums are 'Kati Patang' and 'Hum Kisi Se Kum Nahin' and I love to hum songs like 'O mere dil ke chain' and 'Maine poocha chaand se.' A royal man, Rahul-da was and will always remain the 'maharaja' of filmy gaane.'

LEENA CHANDAVARKAR-GANGULY

FORMER BOLLYWOOD ACTRESS AND WIFE OF LEGENDARY
MULTI-FACETED KISHORE KUMAR

'*Pancham-da bade zinda-dil insaan thhe*—his vibrant voice still keeps ringing in my ears, whenever I recall his frequent visits to our bungalow 'Gauri Kunj' at Juhu (Mumbai). Just the way, he shared a close bonding with my husband 'KK' (Kishore Kumar) and with Amit Kumar, RDB also shared a good rapport with me.

Besides my love for writing lyrics and listening to music, I shared a crazy 'common' interest with Rahul-da—of eating khaana spiced with hot chillies. Such food used to give me a strange 'nashaa' shedding tears. When RDB came to know he would say, we are birds of the same 'pungent' feather and I would laugh heartily. Quite often, the 'Master Chef' Rahul would make us relish the specially prepared fish-kheema dish that he had made for us, using his home-grown chillies. And then he would call us on phone and insist "*chaawal ke saath khaana.*"

Being a sensitive Cancerian, RDB could not bear to see anyone suffering, even domestic pets. When his doggie 'Tipsy' had passed away, RDB was crying copiously. 'In the morning when I left home, I just forgot to caress it,' he said stifling his sobs. That day, by the time he reached home, his pet had breathed its last. We also possessed a smart doggie that we called 'Benny' and Pancham-da had developed a fond attachment even for our pet.

Not many people are aware that I have done three films with music by RDB including the social thriller with the title 'Saas Bhi Kabhi Bahu Thi' (1970). Yet another movie with RDB's music where I played the lead was 'Dil Ka Raaja' (1972). With his kind-hearted, amicable nature I feel Pancham-da was indeed a *"dil ka raja"* whose mission on 'planet earth' was to make music-lovers immensely happy.'

'To just know that Pancham-da 'considered' me for '1942: A Love Story' but couldn't find me, as I was in Delhi, is a magnificent feather in my cap. He passed away before I found my place in the music industry, but he lives through his music and anecdotes in the hearts of every music-lover. 'Amar Prem,' 'Padosan' and 'Teesri Manzil' are some of his many great albums close to my heart.

The song 'Jab hum jawaan honge' from 'Betaab' had a kids' version too, for which we shot. But unfortunately, it wasn't retained in the film due to the length'.

– Sonu Nigam
Eminent pop n'playback singer and composer

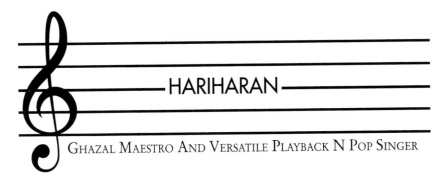

HARIHARAN

GHAZAL MAESTRO AND VERSATILE PLAYBACK N POP SINGER

"A gem of a human being, R D Burman had 'laya,' 'taal' and 'sur' throbbing in his blood and he perfectly knew the pulse of the masses. It was my privilege to sing several playback numbers like the peppy 'Hai mubaarak' (*'Boxer'*) and this popular soulful devotional track 'Mere man mandir' ('Dard Ka Rishta') for Panchamda. In fact, I used to travel with Panchamda and Asha-ji Bhosle a lot for their 'live' concerts and both of them attended my wedding reception. When he heard my 'Sukoon' album, he said, 'this is the kind of harmony I always wanted to use in life.' Then, I had also sung four lovely songs for Dada, in this Amjad Khan production movie which I think was called 'Lambaae Chaudaaee' Or 'Mezaan,' but unfortunately that project got 'shelved.' Very encouraging by nature, he used also say tongue-in-cheek, you are a classically trained singer, but don't show your training while singing. There was this amazing concept he had shared with me on internalising the precise time-count of quantum of seconds to sync with the song-tempo. Interestingly, I sang my version of a few 're-arranged' songs including 'O hansini' and 'Tum bin jaaon khaan' for this tribute-to-RDB movie 'Dil Vil Pyar Vyar.' Genius RDB's retro-music is so fresh and rocking, that it hugely connects with today's EDM-centric youth."

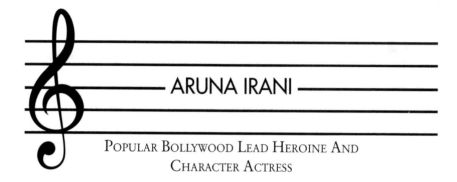

ARUNA IRANI

POPULAR BOLLYWOOD LEAD HEROINE AND
CHARACTER ACTRESS

'Sometimes I feel I have been 'blessed' that I have performed to possibly the widest range and contrasting variety of song situations, all composed by the revered Pancham-da. If a pure classical thumri song 'Hume tumse pyar kitna' sung by Begum Parveen Sultana was picturised on me in 'Kudrat,' in stark contrast I have cavorted to Usha Uthup's Westernized 'One two cha cha cha' in 'Shalimar.' If there is the soul-stirring 'Sapna mera toot gaya' in 'Khel Khel Mein' in which Pancham-da's vibrant voice serenades me with 'Aaja meri baahon mein aa,' there is 'Chadti jawani meri chaal mastani' in 'Caravan' sung by Lata-ji to which I have swung and swayed. In showbiz, some artistes used to point out that I was lucky to get such a colourful assortment of RDB songs.

If I am not mistaken, I guess I must have easily acted in at least thirty-five films (possibly the highest) which has music by R. D. Burman, either as a lead heroine as in 'Bombay to Goa' or as a supporting artiste for dance numbers in movies like 'Deewar.' One of my favorite sentimental songs was 'Kya gazab karte ho jee' from Love Story. It's such an unconventional yet mellifluous foot-tapping melody. I enjoyed dancing and wooing Bunty (Kumar Gaurav) on-screen. The song which I found relatively difficult was 'Dilbar dil se pyare' in 'Caravan.' Honestly, I don't know dancing and there was hardly any time for 'rehearsals.' But the Arabic-gypsy music genre and rhythm of the song which RDB has composed, had such infectious vibes that I would swing and sway gracefully. The award-winning song 'Hume tumse pyar kitna' sung by Begum Parveen picturised on me was rather challenging. There was absolutely no dancing for my character that is shown sitting throughout. Although in real-life, I was in my mid-20s, I was shown as a singer in fifties with grey hair. I had to perfectly match the *murkis* and the *harkats* in the classical *thumri* song with the right facial expressions, hand gestures and lip-sync. Although I never had the opportunity to leisurely sit and chat with RDB, I used to briefly meet him with Asha-ji (Bhosle) sometimes at events and film parties. Invariably I found him unassumingly courteous.'

"All our composed songs are dedicated to the memory of our icon R D Burman, whose diverse repertoire is a 'University' of music. It was our privilege to compose for 'Jhankaar Beats' (2003) directed by Sujoy Ghosh, which was our unique tribute to Panchamda—he will always be a guiding, dazzling 'star.' " –**Shekhar Ravjiani (of Vishal-Shekhar composer duo)**

KAVITA KRISHNAMURTHY

Distinguished Award-Winning Playback
and Concert-Singer

"It's my good fortune that I must have sung at least an aggregate of thirty-five songs for Panchamda with each track being a learning experience. Right from 1980s, I had been seen singing for RDB's movies like 'Boxer,' but none of the songs had attained a cult status. That's when he assured me that it would happen someday and '1942: A Love Story' materialized. When I met 'dada' for this 'period' movie, he told me that it was set in the 'pre-independence' era like 'Bandini.' The first song was 'Dil ne kahaa chupke se,' which when I heard, I frankly told him in a timid tone that this song was ideally suited for Lata-didi's caliber. **It was Pancham-da who instilled courage and confidence in me and said, 'you can and only you will do it—just follow me exactly the way I enunciate the lyrical words and you will score a hit,' he had enthused. The rest is history.**

What was very graceful about Rahul-da *(and even with composer Laxmikant-ji)* was that during any recording, he would never shout or scream - if there were any flaws or errors made by the singers. This was because there were over seventy top acoustic musicians sitting in the large hall. Rather, RDB would personally come to the singer's cabin and gently say, 'Your lines are not coming out well; would you try to modify your tone or improvise a bit?'

Once when all of us went for a live concert in, Bangkok we checked into a restaurant where we were served delicious '*Tomyum*,' a Thai soup. Since Dada was feeling awkward to ask directly, he urged me to ask the Chef to reveal the detailed 'recipe' for that soup, and when I did so, dada noted it all. **A month later, after we returned, RDB had himself prepared the soup and added his own extra ingredients—it had an awesome taste. 'As a creative person, I wished to add my own flavor to it,' shrugged RDB.**

Whether it was at parties, events or backstage, Panchamda was the most 'animated' person I ever saw. **Honestly, I feel that all his life he lived like a '20-year old man'—with that zestful optimistic energy.** Even during his unfavorable phase, when he was out of work, which in turn adversely affected his health, he never divulged his distress but remained cheerful.

Among the various 'Guru-mantras' that he taught me was 'not to worry even if your face gets distorted and you look ugly.' But to 'enunciate'the lyrical words and phrases clearly, to pen your mouth wide for the '*aa-kar*,' '*ee-kar*' and '*oo-kar*' at recordings, and to follow him. Check out my seductive mood song 'Badan mein chandni' in 'Ghaatak,' and see how dada has made me sing with aplomb. As is known, RDB had a supreme sense of rhythm and was also a master at 'syncopating' the beats with the vocals.

To sum up I can say that Pancham-da was an unassuming 'genius' much ahead of his times. Which is why his contrived 'remixes' just do not sound good.'

Composer ANAND

(OF THE FAMOUS DUO 'ANAND-MILIND')

'Even the famous Ripley of 'Believe it or Not' fame would have been hesitant to believe what I am about to share with you. When our musical mega-hit movie 'Qayamat Sey Qayamat Tak (QSQT)' was ready, there were dozens of trial shows (previews) held by 'showman' Nasir Hussain for the prospective film distributors and select showbiz people. When they came out after the screening they would generally shrug. Reacting with lame evasive excuses like *"music thandaa hai"* and *"hero zaraa short hai."* They simply declined to back the film. This was quite distressing for Nasir-saab and director Mansoor Khan, who took it all in their stride.

Then the titan of film-music, R. D. Burman sir got invited for a special trial show of 'QSQT.' As soon as he came out after the screening, he exclaimed loudly, **'superhit music, terrific film;** nobody can stop this amazing music.' **Pancham-da was so charged that he also added, 'Watch my prediction, this music will create havoc.'** That was the first exceptional morale-boosting energy shot-in-the-arm. **Tell me, which music director who has been gracefully 'replaced' by Milind and me, in the prestigious Nasir Hussain banner would have showered such lavish compliments, that too genuinely.** The rest, as they say, is history.

Even when he came for the grand 'QSQT' release event, Pancham-da kept saying to Milind and me, *"Tum logon ki nikall padi."* Be prepared to ride on the waves of success, you won't have time to breathe. With his 'zero-ego' attitude, he kept complimenting Milind and me on the brilliant sound balancing-mixing and music arrangements of 'QSQT.' Coming from the 'Master' himself, we were both overwhelmed and speechless. **So accurate was RDB's advance prophecy that not only did the songs become a hit 'big time,' but 'QSQT' even won the Filmfare Award for the 'Best Music.'**

A year later I had gone to Film Center for some work where I was told that RDB was inside the recording studio. Since there was this board displayed which said 'R. D. Burman recording—No Outsiders Allowed,' I was waiting patiently outside in the access corridor. A while later, Panchamda apparently wanted to go to the wash-room, so he came out and happened to see me. Dada was so unassuming that he straightaway took me inside to the console-room. Incidentally, my dad, music director Chitragupta happened to be a close friend of Sachin Dev Burman, hence our bonding had its roots from the previous generation. **What intrigued me was that the modest RDB was highly curious to know intricate technical details of the way we executed our recording and mixed our music tracks.** Interestingly, the super-proficient Ashok Shukla was our common sound-recordist. All the same, I told him, "*Dada aap hamaare sabke iconic-Boss hai. Itne saalon sey aap hi ke gaane sunkar seekhte aaye hain.*" It turned out to be a very productive discussion where we exchanged notes. At the end of it, both Milind and I have been humbled by the **celebrated composer's quest for excellence,** even after a glorious track-record that includes iconic musical films like 'Hare Rama Hare Krishna,' 'Sholay' and 'Hum Kisi Se Kam Nahin'.'

'R. D. Burman-saab is a legend who was ahead of his time and someone that the new generation looks up to. I must admit that I have been a huge 'fan' of Panchamda and he continues to be my inspiration. Evergreen songs like 'Chura liya,' 'Jab chaha yaara tumhe,' 'O mere sona re,' 'Ae khuda har faisla' and 'O haseena zulfonwali' are some of my favorite tracks from RDB's repertoire and each one of them is a classic masterpiece. Contrary to impressions, I have never tried to imitate or step into Burman-da's shoes—he is an iconic musical legend. My remix duet version (with Asha Bhonsle) of RDB's 'Mehbooba' number in 'Aap Kaa Suroor' and this fusion item-song 'O Balma' from 'Khiladi 786' are among my humble heartfelt on-screen tributes to the maestro. Coincidentally, I scored the innovative music for this movie 'Sanam Teri Kasam' (2016), which also happens to be the title of this landmark retro movie which had fetched Pancham-da his first-ever Filmfare Award in 1983. During my lifetime, if I attain a score of even 20 percent of RDB's versatile genius, I will feel I have fulfilled my musical mission.'

– Himesh Reshammiya
Popular innovative Bollywood music composer-singer and lead actor

'Some divine souls never depart away from us and one amongst them is R. D. Burman Ji. I have grown up listening to Pancham Da's songs. Off the top of my head I can think of 'Tere bina zindagi se koi,' 'Tum bin jaoon kahan,' 'Mehbooba mehbooba' and I can keep going. Pick any song of his, whether it was sad or happy, he made it unique as if he sprinkled life on every piece of work he created. **For me, he will always be the 'God of Retro Music.'** The praises will never end so I would like to conclude by saying 'I won't say we miss you **Pancham Da, I would say you are alive in us and will always be remembered through your music.'**

– Suniel Shetty
Versatile macho Bollywood lead star-actor

Dada fondly called me 'Madonna' because of my golden hair.

'Not just a great composer, RDB was a diligent teacher who taught me that one should not sing just from the throat but deep within from the navel. While recording, he taught me the 'correct' voice-throw technique on the mic. Honestly, I feel I am blessed and honoured that I got to bring out an entire non-filmy album 'Dil Tera Hua' specially composed by R. D. Burman, which had seven duets and one solo all in my voice. The disheartening part is that this private album was released only after Dada passed away. It was at the hands of star-actor Jeetu-ji (Jeetendra), who also is a huge fan of RDB's songs, as Dada has given him such a contrasting variety of chartbuster tracks. Besides this, Dada also made me sing the Bengali movie hit duet song, 'Mone theke mone ki' with Amit Kumar, which is the Bangla version of 'Rooth na jaana.' Way back in '86, when I was absolutely new to showbiz, Pancham-da came and even 'danced' extempore with me on stage, while I was singing at one of the fund-raising cine-industry concerts in Kolkata. It was such a major morale-booster for me. Since my hair used to have a golden shade-colour, RDB had nicknamed me 'Madonna' and he used to fondly call me by that name. Nobody can ever replace him; he was a unique composer and an endearing human being.'

– **Sapna Mukherji**
Pop n' playback singer & music-biz professional

Gimme a Five!

'In consonance with his pet name, Pancham *(fifth note of the scale)*, here are five things that come to my mind. First, assimilate all you can but carve your own identity. Second, labels like 'Western' or 'Indian classical' do not matter for masses remember tunes and not genres. **Next, compose and arrange musical interludes minutely, but always leave enough room for improvisation at the studio.** Fourth, innovate constantly with instruments like bass-guitar, resso resso, castanets, human breath, gurgling, beer bottles, tea cups, saucers and so on. Lastly, let the sounds of nature and folk music be your eternal tune bank.'

–Siraj Syed

Eminent senior music critic and disc jockey

"'Pancham uncle' (as I fondly called him) was a composer far ahead of his times. His songs are evergreen, and he is ONE music director whose songs have been remixed again and again. He created magic with his music. His songs were melodious with pulsating beats; his songs had it all.

I feel I was blessed to have 'sung' for him in films like 'Yaadon Ki Baarat,' 'The Burning Train,' 'Kitaab,' 'Darling Darling,' 'Ishq Ishq Ishq' etc. And I think in one of his last movies, 'Professor Ki Padosan,' in which I acted, I also had the opportunity to 'sing' for him.'

'I never saw him ever get angry or excited. He was an extremely warm, humble and a loving human being. He is terribly, terribly missed by one and all even today. That's the impact he left on people. His songs still haunt me, make me get up and dance, and make me sing-along. He will always be missed for generations to come. My favorite three RDB songs are 'Ek baat dil mein ayi hai' from 'Rahi Badal Gaye,' 'Bolo bolo kuch toh bolo' from 'Zamaane Ko Dikhana Hai'and 'Aa mulakaton ka mausam agaya' from 'Lovers.'"

– Padmini Kolhapure - Sharma

Highly talented former Bollywood lead actress and a wonderful
singer

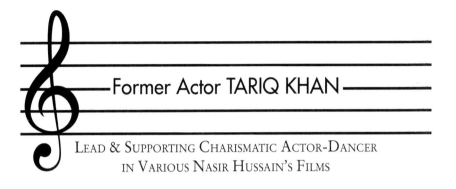

Former Actor TARIQ KHAN

LEAD & SUPPORTING CHARISMATIC ACTOR-DANCER
IN VARIOUS NASIR HUSSAIN'S FILMS

*Who happens to be mega-star Aamir Khan's first cousin,
takes off literally into a 'yaadon ki baarat.'*

'Frankly speaking, 95 percent of my success as a 'dancing rockstar'
goes to composer R. D. Burman and showman Nasir Hussain-
saab who is my maternal uncle. That's because I got hijacked into
movies by default. By nature I was shy, reserved and introvert and
did not know either acting or formal dancing. Even when I went to
an acting academy I was shunted out, because the instructors felt I
was 'just not cut out for showbiz.' Once Nasir-saab happened to see
me dance like crazy, at one of our family social events and he made a
mental note of it. That's when he offered me the third hero's singer-
dancer character in the Dharmendra-starrer 'Yaadon Ki Baarat,' which
eventually emerged a 'diamond jubilee' mega musical hit. Besides the
title-song, the chartbuster dance duet numbers like 'Aapke kamre mein
koi,' 'Dil mil gaye' and 'Lekar hum deewana' were picturised mainly
on me and some portions on Zeenat Aman and Vijay Arora. Before
the songs were even shot, Pancham-uncle boosted my morale as he
said excitedly, *"Gaane bahut hi kamaal ke ban gaye hain. Ab tumko
super-kamaal screen-performance dena hoga. Jo tum kar sakte ho."*

Then came, 'Hum kisi se kum nahin' yet again a jubilee mega-
hit. Exults Tariq, whose musical idol is Elvis Presley. It was such an

privilege that Nasir-saab made me perform in the unique competition-song, but **I also had the great honour of having Mohammed Rafi-saab sing that iconic song 'Kya hua tera vaada' which was picturised on me. When I came to know that this song merited a Filmfare Award as well as the coveted National Award for Rafi-saab, I was so thrilled. But sadly, Pancham-uncle was ignored in the award-winners that year. Yet another feather in my career cap was that this chartbuster song 'Tum kya jaano mohabbat kya hai' sung by Pancham-da was picturised on me.** This Western flavor song was choreographed by the dance-master Suresh Bhatt in a 'unique' way, where he also made me 'kneel' on the stage with one hand-palm on my ear and sing—as if it was a fusion-qawaali. **During this song I was instructed to keep a 'paan-wrap' in my mouth—so that my mouth-lip movements could match Pancham's high octave notes in the overture, 'OooooooooHo—Tum kya jaano.' Since I had seen RDB's 'Mehbooba mehbooba' visual many times, I could manage to put in my best. Since there were many retakes, I must have munched at least ten 'paan' wraps during that shoot, laughs the actor,** who later used to host his own musical shows 'Tariq Nites' which were sell-outs. "Salaam Panchamda", he signs off.

Tailpiece: Making his screen-debut as a child-actor, the 'cho-chweet' Aamir Khan incidentally played the young child actor who grows up to be Tariq in 'Yaadon Ki Baaraat' and can be seen on-screen zestfully humming the title song. 'Perfectionist' Aamir has very high regards for R. D. Burman. And the innovative composer is among the Khan's all-time favourite 'top-ten' luminaries in Bollywood.

JATIN (SATISH) WAGLE

<ruby label="ACCLAIMED MAVERICK MARATHI FILM-MAKER">ACCLAIMED MAVERICK MARATHI FILM-MAKER</ruby>

Why did R. D. Burman refuse to take a single rupee for scoring the music of the musical hit 'Namak Haram,' starring Rajesh Khanna and Amitabh Bachchan?

Jatin (Satish) Wagle converses exclusively with the Author

Q -Your late father Satish Wagle, who had co-produced the superhit musical 'Namak Haram' (1973) starring two superstars, Rajesh Khanna and Amitabh Bachchan, had told me once that R. D. Burman never used to accept any professional fee for scoring the music for all his productions, including his Marathi TV serial and Marathi movie. Would you elaborate on this magnanimous gesture?

Jatin- 'It's a very interesting but a l-o-n-g story, but I will share it with you in brief. It's true that Pancham-da never ever took money from my dad (Satish Wagle). My dad's previous two co-productions, 'Pyar Hi Pyar' and 'Yaar Mera,' had their music scored by the famous musicians, Shankar-Jaikishan. Being a very close friend of my father, the legendary Jaikishan never charged professional fee for both those films. At the same time, dad also shared a warm rapport with Pancham-da. After Jaikishan's untimely death, my dad approached Shanker-ji, but he insisted that RDB should be taken on board as the music director of 'Namak Haram.'

'What flummoxed my dad was that even after 'Namak Haram' became a musical superhit, and my father had tried to coax RDB to accept a decent amount, he simply refused. There was a rationale behind Pancham-uncle's refusal. He told my dad: 'Had Jaikishan been alive, you would not have come to me. If Jaikishan had continued working with you, he would not have accepted his remuneration from you. Now that you have come to me, it means I am the next choice, the replacement for Jai (kishan). So I feel I have no right to charge money just because Jai is no more. Let us continue the non-commercial bonding tradition.'

'Not only that, the ethical RDB was so particular that he accompanied my dad to obtain prior permission from composer Shankar-ji permitting him (RDB) to take charge of the banner's music department, even before they had started the recording of 'Namak Haram.' How many such instances have we heard in music-biz? What a mind-blowing score he came up with for the landmark that movie starring the two superstars, Rajesh Khanna and Amitabh Bachchan. Even for the subsequent projects that my dad produced, which included the film 'Naukri,' a Marathi TV serial called 'Yaala Jeevan Aise Naav' and a Marathi movie called 'Sukhi Sansaarachi Baara Sutre,' Pancham-uncle never charged a single rupee. The sentimental RDB seemed passionate towards musical notes with no craze for currency notes. Now, will someone tell me where we can find such 'selfless Samaritans' in today's showbiz?'

'Contrary to speculations that Pancham was location-scouting for some Marathi movie in Pune on 3 January 1994, to the best of my knowledge, he was very much in Mumbai. That's because we were in Pune in those days and are still based in Pune. And on 3 January, in the afternoon, RDB interacted with us from Bombay via his landline phone when he called my mother (Pratim) and spoke to her in fluent Marathi, addressing her as 'wainee' (bhabhi). My mother was initially perplexed, but then she realized who it was. In fact my father who had gone out then came back home and called him up to inform him that the 'Madhur Dhwani' recording studios in Mumbai had been booked from January 7 to 10 for the song recording of 'Sukhi Sansarchi Baara Sutre,' directed by Anil Baindur. The songs were to be sung by Suresh

Wadkar and Asha Bhosle. One song was to be sung by debutant singer Vijay Joshi from Pune. My dad had actually gone to Bombay the next day, i.e. on 4 January, to set up all the necessary arrangements for the recordings. But the tragic twist was that he went to Marylands, in a state of utter shock and disbelief, to attend RDB's funeral.

Weeks after the legend had passed away, my dad felt the 'RDB show must go on,' and we took the timely help of melody queen Asha-tai Bhosle and master musician Ranjit 'Kancha' Gazmer to complete the recording of all the songs of the Marathi film. A few tunes had already been composed, but the rest were finalized by director Anil from RDB's stock-tunes, which had been provided to us. One of the songs was sung by debutant singer Vijay Joshi from Pune.'

'Band of Boys' pop-singer CHIN2 BHOSLE-

(GRANDSON OF LEGENDARY SINGER ASHA BHOSLE)

Q &A

How has Pancham-da's influence inspired your singing as a pop singer-composer?

- I love the way he could bring world music into his compositions. He loved to listen to music that was composed worldwide and would devour world music during his travels or on LPs/cassettes.

- Anything that could produce a sound was a potential instrument. It's very difficult to compose music without boundaries, and here's one man who effortlessly did that. A glass and a spoon, breathing, two sticks found on the road they all sang to him!

- His musical interludes totally do it for me! Many songs are made in a typical format—mukhda-cross-mukhda-musical interlude-antra-mukhda-musical interlude and so on. Often a composer includes the interlude because 'that's the way it's done' and 'something needs to be there after the singer has finished singing his bit.' And if you listen carefully, you can hear that very intent! With RDB it's just different. The musical interlude doesn't sound like it's there because it needs to be. The space he fills with the interlude takes you to a different level all together and brings you back to the song when the singer returns. You are very much influenced by him when you listen to his music!

Eminent music critics say that RDB's classic chartbusters (like 'Dum maro dum') should ideally never be 'remixed.' What is your take on this?

- That's like saying the pizza should be eaten only in its original form! It's only when you experiment that you get to eat the classic dish in various new forms and flavors—some variants you relish and some you don't, but then that's a personal choice, isn't it? If 'remix' is a way to bring an old melody to the ears of today's generation, then so be it! The purists may not like the way it's been done. But you really need to turn your attention towards the listener and see the joy it brings them! Is that wrong? I'm all for music reaching out to as many people as it can. Just give the original composer/artist the due credit!!

What according to you makes rockstar RDB a unique, versatile, timeless (evergreen) and genius composer? Can you give a brief analysis, preferably with examples of songs?

- His breakaway and experimenting psyche that is evident in the song 'Lekar hum diwana dil' from the movie Yaadon Ki Baaraat. Listen to the intro, and you will know what I'm talking about. It's totally unconventional. It's a peep into the mind of a genius and an eccentric! Rhythm changes, melody changes, instrument experimenting and so on. It's not just an intro but words being spoken (for those listening!).

- His unreal grasp of melodies, for example 'Ek ladki ko dekha' from the movie '1942: A Love Story.' The entire song has the same awesome melody running through it for four minutes! But very few realise it. There has to be genius there!

- His ability to make the complex sound simple, for example 'Oh hansini' from the movie 'Zahreela Insaan.' I totally love the way it's got a minor-major shift in the melody line. I had composed a song with the same shift, and no singer was happy with the way they had to shift modes (or raagas from an Indian perspective). But these same singers would sing 'Oh hansini,' without realizing the shift, and go *"wah wah." That is something only Pancham-da can do!*

As a kid and teenager which were some of your favorite RDB compositions?

- Dil lena khel hai—it has so much fun and movement happening!
- Jahan teri ye nazar—the guitar strumming caught me from bar 1 onwards!
- Bachna ae haseeno—Total energy in the music!

Which RDB composition tracks would you have loved to sing as a playback under him?

Piya tu—Ooooh so many colours to that song, the James Bond feel, the breathing, and the beginning rhythm. Just crooning 'Monica' would be enough!

Jaane jaan—Again with my legendary grandmom (Asha Bhosle). I would love to experiment with the harmony vocals, which run so hauntingly with the main melody line!

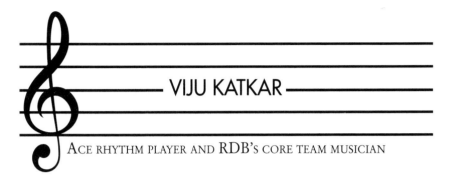

VIJU KATKAR

ACE RHYTHM PLAYER AND RDB'S CORE TEAM MUSICIAN

'Had it not been for my mentor and guru Pancham-da, I would have ended up being either a 'master tailor' or a 'still-video photographer.' This is despite the fact that I am the son of the veteran master percussionist-tabla player Amrutrao Katkar, who was part of RBD's core team of musicians. I had repeatedly failed in my final school exams, so I decided to acquire some skills other than playing musical instruments. Rhythm runs in my blood genetically, and I had imbibed the rudiments of tabla playing from my father during my childhood and teenage phase.

It was part of my routine to deliver my father's lunch to the Film Center at RDB's recordings so that he could have his lunch by 2pm after the session or during the break. RDB observerd me carefully, and after I had left asked my father whether I was a scholar at studies. **When my father said that I was a 'flop' in my studies, and that I wished to take up tailoring, RDB chuckled and said, "Kal se mere sitting mein bhej dena." When my dad probed as to why he wanted me, he said jestfully, *"Mere kapde wohi seelayega."*** When my father came home, he called me right away and said, 'Dada has called you tomorrow for his music session.' There was a mixed reaction of anxiety and excitement at my end because I was unaware as to what was in store for me.

At RDB's sitting room the next day, only his core musicians and Asha-tai were present. When he announced that I would be joining his team, Asha-tai said it was too early to induct me as *"abhi to uske padhaai ke din hain."* But Pancham-da was adamant and said he could 'sense' that I had 'inherited rhythm' from my father. So I was summoned to the recording 'take,' where on the first day I was asked to play the standing 'Urdu' dholak on the bass side. It was the song recording of 'Yeh vaada raha,' and I contributed to the sharp dafli-like sound beats of that racy duet song 'Ishq meri bandagi hai.' RDB used to come from behind, put his hand on my shoulder and say *"bajao Viju dilse bajao."* What more could I ask for? My music career was being 'tailor-made' under the scrutiny of the boss himself.

Thereafter I became part of the 'Pancham parivaar' and was asked to regularly play the tabla, or the conga or the tumba and even created bizarre sound effects in some of his songs. **I still remember when Amitabh Bachchan sir was present at the 'Mahaan' recording. In that fast-paced song 'Yeh din toh aata hai,' I was instructed by RDB to tap a suspended metal gong plate while dipping it and lifting it alternately in a vessel filled with water. After the 'take' Bachchan saab seemed quite amused and glanced at me with appreciation. Then there was that song 'Reshmi zulfein' from 'Indrajeet.' For the opening prelude of this track, RDB specially asked me to fetch a 'key-operated clockwork toy' and produce that weird whirr-tik-tak sound.** Of the hundreds of songs that I played, my favourites are the two fusion numbers 'Aisa samaa na hota' (Zameen Aasmaan) and 'Jaane do naa' (Saagar) and the ghazal 'Huzur is kadar bhi' (Masoom). **Dada was so fond of me that he coaxed me to face the camera and play a 'tabalchi' in the movie 'Alag Alag,' where Rajesh Khanna plays the role of a 'singer.' This scene was picturized inside RDB's Marylands flat. On the day of the shoot, he told me,** *"Tension mat lena, tumko to sirf imaandaari se bajaana hai, acting thodi na karni hai."* My *yaadon ki baraat* can go on for weeks; but I guess some of the glimpses I have shared will help unravel the mystique behind the legendary Rahul-da, who was and is a superhuman wonder.'

RANJIT 'KAANCHA' GAZMER

ACE PERCUSSIONIST MAADAL PLAYER AND RDB'S CORE TEAM MUSICIAN

'Even when I did not play 'maadal' for eight months at RDB's recordings, the benevolent boss would send me my remuneration regularly,' recalls Ranjit 'Kaancha' Gazmer, as he unravels the mystery behind Pancham-da's 'signature sounds.'

'Rahul-da was not just a genius composer-singer but was a happy-go-lucky yet benevolent human being,' recalls percussionist-composer Ranjit Gazmer fondly. Continues the seventy-five-year-old Gazmer, 'Since I hail from Darjeeling and had mastered Nepali rhythm instruments like the 'maadal,' RDB inducted me into his music team starting from 'Hare Rama Hare Krishna (1971), and he fondly nicknamed me 'Kaancha.' There was a crisis in my career in the 1970s **after a spinal surgery. I was bedridden for eight months. Consequently I was unable to report for all the recordings during my 'sick leave.' But Pancham-da used to send his man almost daily to my house with the remuneration amount, as if I had played in the recording 'take' at Film Center.** Not only that, Dada would often call me up to check my progress, and Asha-didi (Bhosle) would also drop in to meet me,' discloses Kaancha, wiping his trickling tears.

But then, considering that the **"taah-tunng" signature sounds on the 'maadal' were mandatory for RDB songs,** what was the solution that the composer worked out in his absence? 'No, he did not hire any other musician to play the 'maadal' but waited patiently. **After I fully recovered, Dada made play the 'maadal' beats for a series of recordings and dubbed them into nearly fifty songs.** For a few 'urgent' song tracks which could not wait, he had asked Homi-da Mullan to play the similar sounds on the 'duggi' drums.'

My first introduction to Pancham-da was thanks to his chief assistant Manohari-da Singh, during the 'song sittings' of 'Hare Rama Hare Krishna (HRHK).'

It was a divine coincidence that the movie 'HRHK' had Kathmandu as its backdrop. My active association as a core team musician continued for over two decades with RDB, right up to '1942: A Love Story' (1993), he recalls wistfully. Wasn't it a fact that Pancham-da was highly enamoured with the 'maadal beats'? 'Absolutely true!' says Ranjit. 'That 'taah-tunng' was Pancham-da's 'signature sound.' You can distinctly hear my rhythm beats in hundreds of chartbuster songs like 'Hai rey ghungroo' and 'I love you' (both from 'HRHK'), and 'Hum dono do premi' (Ajnabee). Once before the actual 'sitting' began, ace guitarist Bhanu-da Gupta and I were just casually 'jamming' together at RDB's residence. Apparently, dada overheard us and told me to continue playing. Even as he was 'overhearing' our casual masti-bharaa jamming, out of the blue he conjured up the tune and conveyed to Gulzar-saab to book the recording studio. **That's how this classical number 'Tere bina jiya' (Ghar) was born,** where the maverick **RDB made me 'experiment' with varying metallic sound double beats on multiple maadal drums throughout the unique song. Everyone complimented me saying that I had made my maadal 'sing' in this track.** But the credit goes to dada for conceiving the haunting tune and making us play so innovatively. **It was an euphoric experience when I played for the stereophonic, iconic songs of 'Sholay,' 'Jab Taak Hai Jaan' and 'Mehbooba Mehbooba,"** smiles the talented Ranjit, who has 'independently' scored music for 116 Nepali films and has even made Asha Bhosle sing Nepali songs. **'My biggest regret is that I did not muster up the courage to coax and cajole RDB to sing at least one Nepali song.'**

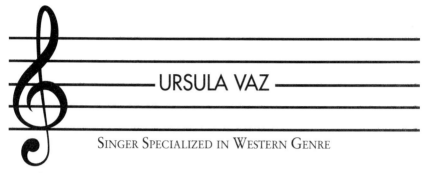

She sang the English song 'I am falling in love with a stranger'
(Deewaar)— the lyrics written by RDB

Q & A

Were you aware that it was composer R. D. Burman who had
written the English lyrics of the song *'I am falling in love
with a stranger' from the landmark movie 'Deewaar'?*

Strangely no! Now that I know, I am enlightened. But then I am
also wondering why Mr. Rahul sir did not disclose that he was the
lyricsist. In fact I presumed that the famous lyricist Sahir Ludhianvi
must have also written these verses as well. Possibly RDB was so
engrossed in the Brazilian style bossa nova flavor and jazzy composing
arranging aspects that he forgot to mention it to me. Or maybe since
he was so unassuming, he preferred to be discreet.

It's only in the past ten years that people have realized that an
Indian singer (me) and not a foreign artiste has sung this track. Would
you believe it if I told you that **while recording this song I was
unaware on whom the song would be picturized? It's only when I
got to watch 'Deewaar' that I realized my track starts when Parveen
Babi is trying to make amorous advances to Amitabh Bachchan's
debonair don's character at the luxurious hotel's cocktail bar!**

Do you recall your experiences of your song session with Pancham-da?

The day before the recording I was called to Film Center for rehearsals in the presence of Pancham-da, and he seemed impressed with my voice and also my la-la-la-la improvisations, as he wanted that 'foreign' intonation and perfect English accent. Actually, it was my first 'solo' song recording. I am a live-band crooner, and incidentally I am not a formally trained singer. But then I happened to be the daughter of eminent trumpet player and music arranger 'Chic Chocolate' (Anthony Vaz), who actively assisted composers C. Ramchandra and even O. P. Nayyar. On the day of the recording, RDB confirmed the 'key-scale' of my vocal tonal notes. We recorded a couple of 'takes' and an elated RDB later said 'very nice, you sang exactly the way I wanted it.' By nature, the genius RDB was jolly, friendly and courteous. Some years later, RDB once again called me to record only the English lyrics 'We are two love birds - hum tum do raahi' for a song. It was a Hindi duet number with the fabulous singer S. P. Balasubramaniam in this movie titled 'Yeh Toh Kamaal Ho Gaya.' My voice was used for some foreign actress paired opposite Kamal Hassan in that movie.

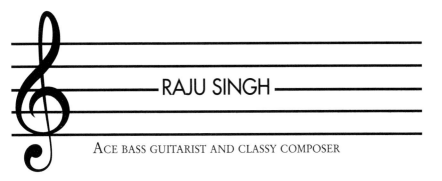

RAJU SINGH

ACE BASS GUITARIST AND CLASSY COMPOSER

'It seems as if Pancham-da has planned it from up there'

'With the previous proposed release dates, which were tossed and shuffled between August and October, getting cancelled, the 3D version of 'Sholay' finally released on 3 January 2014. It gives me goosebumps, because it was just a day prior to the twentieth death anniversary (January 4) of legendary 'Sholay' music director Rahul Dev Burman. **It seems as if Pancham-da had planned it from up there,**' says melody wizard Raju Singh, who was assigned the ultra tough task of 'recreating' the film audio tracks of 'Sholay 3D' in its stereophonic version.

A euphoric Raju reacts, 'It's all thanks to Pancham-da's blessings, the timely references of Javed Akhtar saab, my associate sound designers **Kunal Mehta and Parikshit Lalwani,** and of course the presenter **Jayantibhai Gada's** approval that I have been assigned the challenging responsibility of recreating the background music sound tracks of this cult classic movie. We have used the latest multidimensional **'Dolby Atmos'** surround sound acoustics for 'Sholay 3D.' We have tried our very best to perfectly replicate all the background instrumental sounds. Some of them quite bizarre, like using the metal ball from underneath the chassis of a truck, just the way the boss RDB had done in the original. No, we haven't touched the dialogues or the vocal tracks. It's heartening that the enterprising co-producers Sascha, Shehzad and Shaan from the Sippy clan are delighted with our diligent efforts.' Raju, whose actual name is Rajender, is an expert guitar player and had the privilege of playing 'bass guitar' for RDB's song 'takes' and background scores for nearly seven years up to 1993. Reliving the past, Raju explains, 'Since my dad Charanjit Singh, who is an acclaimed electronic keyboard player, used to regularly play for RDB's recordings, as a kid, I used to accompany him. That's how Pancham-da became fond of me and pampered me with chocolates always.'

HEMANT KENKRE

MUSIC AND RHYTHM CONNOISSEUR AND AD-BIZ
PROFESSIONAL

Bonding with Big Band

'It would be a no-brainer to say that Pancham Uncle *(so proud to call him that)* was skewed towards Latin and Afro-Caribbean sounds. Most of his hit compositions were based on that genre. To me, two other influences that he nurtured stood out namely the Big Band Jazz and his love for signature songs from the James Bond movies.

In the song 'O hansini,' the opening two words were inspired by the song from Goldfinger. The rest of the song is his maverick composition. The 'pum pum pum' interlude of 'Koi diya jale kahin'(Dil Padosi Hai)and 'Mera pyaar shalimar'could have well been used in a typical Bond titles scene. His gruff 'Meri jaan maine kaha' is a tribute to the legendary Louis Armstrong's 'We have all the time in the world' from 'On Her Majesty's Secret Service'—not the melody but the gruff intonation by Pancham Uncle.

Big Band Jazz, particularly the brass section, influenced him to create gems like 'Tum jaison ko toh paayal main baandh loon'(Garam Masala) and the lesser known 'Lo mera pyaar le lo'(Nafrat). One can imagine the electrifying atmosphere in the recording hall when top notch musicians gathered to add garnish to Pancham Uncle's creations. It must have been a super magical experience!'

'While many listeners associate R. D. Burman with peppy, Western-influenced numbers and evergreen love songs, **the truth is that he also used many Hindustani classical raags in his songs.** And it's not something he developed over time. In his debut film *Chhote Nawab* in 1961, he chose the raag Malgunji for the Lata Mangeshkar song 'Ghar aaaja ghir aayi badra.'

Numerous other instances exist. In **Amar Prem**, Pancham-da used the raag Khamaj in two songs, 'Kuchh to log kahenge' and 'Bada natkhat hai.' His 'Raina beeti jaaye' in the same film was an innovative blend of the raagas Todi and Khamaj.

Other famous examples are the hit songs such as 'Beeti na beetayi raina' in raag Yaman Kalyan from Parichay, the **Mehbooba** song 'Mere naina saawan bhadon' in raag Shivranjini and the **Kudrat** masterpiece 'Humein tumse pyaar kitnaa' in raag Bhairavi. **Even the purists applauded his perfection.'**

– Narendra Kusnur

Eminent music columnist and musicologist

NARENDRA KUSNUR

NOTED MUSIC COLUMNIST AND MUSICOLOGIST,

An ardent RDB fan**, goes on a freak fantasy trip — with no malice meant against anyone.

DJ-wale dude takes a U-turn thanks to RDB

'On 31 December 2015, RDB is getting ready for the grand new year party in heaven when he hears his song 'Pyaar humein kis mod pe le aaya.' He looks around to see who's playing it, but then he realises it is being played somewhere very far away, probably on planet earth. He soon figures that it's not the original version he had composed, because it has too many extra beats, funny rap interludes and even heavy metal guitar.

Perplexed, he goes to earth to investigate. His sense of sound takes him to Mumbai, and in his new avataar, he is sporting designer glasses. He meets a groovy twenty-four-year-old international DJ Spin-Stir, who greets him with a 'Yo, who're you? You look somewhat familiar.'

'Doesn't matter. This song you're playing is very different from the original,' replies RDB, as he hears a distorted version of 'Hum dono do premi.' Spin-Stir tells him, 'You seem to be old-fashioned. Ever heard of boss R. D. Burman, the genius? I am remixing his songs.'

'I see,' says RDB, requesting the DJ to allow him to use his console. Soon RDB begins playing the remixed songs and, in barely a few minutes, converts them back to their original form. 'Chief, that's awesome! How did you manage that?' asks Spin-Stir.

Meanwhile, a desi contemporary singer and a film song composer enter the pub. They keep gazing at RDB and just can't believe their eyes! They touch his feet. Spin-Stir realizes who the 'chief' was and collapses.

Today, the 'DJ-wale dude' has joined Burman-da for a sound track restoring-retrieval course as Pancham is teaching him how to compose original music. Finally RDB Boss, DJ ko *"sahi mod pe le aaya"*!'

'Bhajan Samrat' ANUP JALOTA

PROFICIENT BHAJAN, CLASSICAL AND GHAZAL SINGER AND COMPOSER

'Pancham-da's passionate love for classical music is evident in his 'pure' raga-based compositions. It is my privilege that I got to sing this fabulous classical duet song, with Lata-Didi, composed by him which goes, 'Mile jhoom ke, milan ritu aaee' based on raga Darbari. It's from the movie 'Professor Ki Padosan' (finally released in 1993) and my voice is picturised on legendary actor Sanjeev Kumar. This was supposedly the last movie which Sanjeev-ji acted in, before he passed away in 1985. Some of RDB's classical gems were also sung by noted classical singers like 'late' Manna Dey, my close friend Bhupinder Singh and even Begum Parveen Sultana. We will always respect and remember Rahul Dev for his 'a-class-apart' work. My favourite RDB composition is 'Humey tumse pyaar kitna' (raag Shivranjani).'

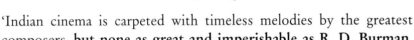

'Indian cinema is carpeted with timeless melodies by the greatest composers, **but none as great and imperishable as R. D. Burman. His music has far outlived the immortal tunes of other composers.** Besides the staggering range of music from the mellow raga-based 'Raina beeti jaye' to the upbeat tempo-driven, chic and urbane 'Yeh ladka haye Allah kaisa hai deewana,' RDB epitomises the very essence of Hindi film music. His music was not only much ahead of its times but also unbeatably exuberant and infinite in its appeal. Emerging from his formidable father's shadows, **RDB went on to achieve much**

more than what the senior Burman had achieved. And that's a fact that even his father would have proudly acknowledged. **First there is the rich heritage of Hindi film music. Then there is R. D. Burman.'**

– Subhash K. Jha

Distinguished music-savvy senior film journalist

'R D Burman—the name is synonymous with creation of magic. Composer RDB was much ahead of his times; an extraordinary music director. **But to me, he was an inventor who sensed music even in a resounding slap, the ignition of a car engine or the morning bell chimes at a temple.** Along with Rajesh Khanna, he was instrumental in getting Kishore Kumar's singing career back on track. It is a mystery why awards eluded him. **But make no mistake of the fact that his music was first rate.** Often criticized for his favouritism towards Western music, it must be said that he also conjured memorable numbers based solely on Indian classical music with equal ease.'

– Bipin R. Pandit

COO, The Advertising Club and Founder of 'Khumaar' musical concerts

'It was at Dev Anand's penthouse that I remember meeting the musical legend Pancham-da. He was sharing with me how Dev-saab was skeptical that the melody of 'Dum maro dum' did not have any Indian-ness to it and could be disliked by the audiences who were used to the S. D. Burman kind of ethnic songs under the Navketan banner. That's when RDB specially composed the Indian melody 'Dekho o deewano,' which immediately follows the 'DMD' song. What I observed was that RDB had an immense respect for Dev-saab and would try to convince him in a courteous manner.

During recordings, **I observed that RDB would be the motivating force in getting the best out of his singers.** The alert composer that he was, he would always try to produce sounds from 'anything' that attracted his attention. In the 1990s, I remember Dev-saab was concerned about RDB's health and wanted him to abstain from heavy drinking, since the latter had recurring cardiac problems. One really wishes that **Dada could have ideally been more health-conscious and lived a much longer life.'**

— Ram Jawhrani

Chairman - Sahyog Foundation and a close associate of the late legendary actor-director Dev Anand

'Every year right up to 1993, the unassuming Pancham-da used to call me up at midnight on 26 June or early morning on 27 June to wish me on my birthday. Then I would reciprocate and wish him. **It was a divine coincidence that both of us shared the same birthday.** Although I did try hard to be the first to wish him, he mostly beat me to it.

Sharing the same birthday, we were similar in nature as both of us were sensitive, jovial, good at mimicking and loved good food besides, of course, the passion for music.

We were both worthy sons of legendary fathers—my dad was Mukesh-ji, and he was the son of S. D. Burman-da. Just as his father had given my dad iconic songs like 'O jaane wale ho sakey,' even Pancham-da gave my father some nineteen songs, including ever-sparkling gems such as 'Ek din bik jaayega' and 'Jiss gali mein mera ghar.' **What is amazing is that RDB always composed soothing, soulful melodies thus allowing Mukesh-ji** to retain his signature style and stamp. **Unfortunately I got to sing only a couple of good songs under RDB's baton.**

Now that Pancham-da has soared into eternal fame, I have been 'missing' his birthday-wish calls.'

— Nitin Mukesh

Eminent Hindi film senior playback singer

'The pioneers who laid the foundation for Bollywood film song formats are the music maestros R.C. Boral and Pankaj Mullick. It is well-known that Rai Chand Boral introduced 'playback' singing in 1935 with the film 'Dhoop Chaaon.' But I can vouch that the legendary R. D. Burman was the 'last of the great lot' in the post-1970s–1980s film music era. He was unnecessarily labelled as a Western music composer when he had composed dozens of classical raga-based chartbusters, especially in Gulzar-saab-directed movies. Like Naushad-saab and Jagjit Singh-ji, Pancham-da too was an *'Ustaad'* in sound design, balancing and mixing. The 'clean, clutter-free sound' in his songs is commendable. Although I grew up on the RDB-Rajesh Khanna combination of breezy hummable melodies, my favourite is Rafi-saab's version of 'Tum bin jaaon kahaan.''

– **Tushar Bhatia**

Eminent music composer, musicologist and sitarist

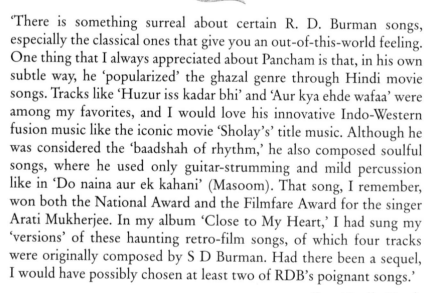

'There is something surreal about certain R. D. Burman songs, especially the classical ones that give you an out-of-this-world feeling. One thing that I always appreciated about Pancham is that, in his own subtle way, he 'popularized' the ghazal genre through Hindi movie songs. Tracks like 'Huzur iss kadar bhi' and 'Aur kya ehde wafaa' were among my favorites, and I would love his innovative Indo-Western fusion music like the iconic movie 'Sholay's' title music. Although he was considered the 'baadshah of rhythm,' he also composed soulful songs, where he used only guitar-strumming and mild percussion like in 'Do naina aur ek kahani' (Masoom). That song, I remember, won both the National Award and the Filmfare Award for the singer Arati Mukherjee. In my album 'Close to My Heart,' I had sung my 'versions' of these haunting retro-film songs, of which four tracks were originally composed by S D Burman. Had there been a sequel, I would have possibly chosen at least two of RDB's poignant songs.'

– 'Late' **Jagjit Singh**

Classical and ghazal maestro, who had spoken to this author in January 2009

'It's my privilege that I have sung playback tracks for the **music maestro, Oscar awardee A R Rahman-Sir** for nearly twenty-five films, including Hindi, Tamil, Telugu and Kannada regional films. The **modest** 'Mozart of Madras,' as he is fondly called, generally prefers to record at least one off-beat, different, experimental type of song in my voice in each of his films. Having said this, **I wish to also share that it's my sheer bad luck that I could not get to sing even a single song composed by the legendary R. D. Burman, as 'dada' had already passed away when I entered music-biz in the mid-1990s. But I got the golden opportunity to sing at the prestigious 'Pancham Platinum' live concert convened by Nitin Shankar to mark RDB's seventy-fifth anniversary.** I sang a few of RDB's evergreen popular songs like 'Aao na gale lagao na' and 'Dum maro dum,' which merited a thundering applause from the audience. This was my token tribute to dada's memory. Honestly, there is no need to remix any of genius RDB's songs, because they all sound as if they were recorded just a few months ago.'

– Madhushree

Eminent versatile playback and pop singer

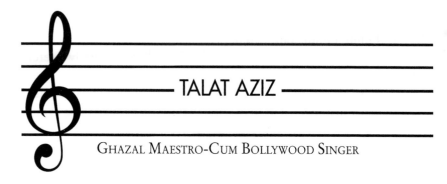

TALAT AZIZ

Ghazal Maestro-Cum Bollywood Singer

US-based NRI audiences go 'ga ga' over RDB chartbusters

'Undoubtedly, composer Pancham-da is a musical icon whose retro songs are a 'rage' among the thousands of NRIs across the globe. **The US-based NRIs were so enthused about the chartbuster yesteryear filmy solos and duets sung by legendary Asha Bhosle, under the baton of R. D. Burman.** In this 'Iconic Tour' series of 'sell-out' concerts across the six prime US cities including **Atlanta, Chicago, San Jose, Dallas, Houston and New Jersey,** Asha-ji and I paid our vocal tributes to the various legendary Bollywood composers, lyricists and singers. This included Rafi-saab, Kishore-da, Mukesh-saab and also the iconic Lata-didi. **The 'ageless' Asha-ji would at times conclude the finale singing and dancing to the sensational all-time pub and party favorites 'Dum maro dum' and 'Piya tu ab toh aaja,' both composed by Pancham-da. The enthused overseas audiences would invariably love to join in.**

We actually created musical history across the US with our sentimental *'salaam'* to Bollywood retro music icons. Melody queen Asha Bhosle and her impresario son Anand (Nandu) Bhosle both endorse this fact.

We were supported by an orchestra of top acoustic musicians conducted by rhythm master Nitin Shanker. My wife, Bina Aziz, had put diligent efforts into the hi-tech backdrop audio-visual showmanship, even as we were performing in some of the prestigious performing arts centres in the US. When I sang popular RDB solo numbers like the peppy 'Yeh shaam mastani' and the soulful 'Tujhse naaraz nahin zindagi,' there was a frenzied response from the audiences. To mark the then ongoing Raksha Bandhan festival, I had also complied with the fervent request to sing the evergreen RDB number 'Phoolon ka taaron ka.'

An uncanny coincidence was that prior to our departure to the US, the 'song rehearsals' were held at the Marylands Apartments in Santacruz (Mumbai). Yes, it was the same apartment where the legendary, late R D Burman had resided and had his iconic song sittings.'

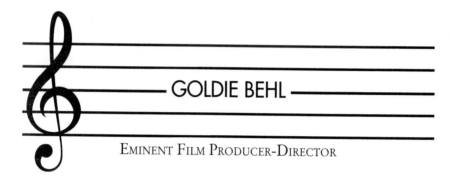

GOLDIE BEHL

EMINENT FILM PRODUCER-DIRECTOR

'Besides being such a hugely talented genius composer-singer, Pancham-uncle was more like a 'father figure' to me. **Since he did not have children of his own, he always treated me like his son and showered me with affection.** As is known to all retro-music lovers, my eminent film-maker father Ramesh ('Gogi') Behl and RDB were very close buddies. And unto his last film, my dad was loyal to him and worked with him in all our home-banner 'Rose Movies' projects. During our own movie recordings at Film Center, I remember Pancham-uncle earnestly showing me around and acquainting me with the musical instruments and the huge mixing console. **When Pancham-uncle passed away on 4 January 1994, it was yet another shattering shock for me and my family. Just four years ago, on 5 January 1990, my dad had passed away.** Now this time, it was RDB who had left us. Since he was like my father, they asked me to perform the *"antim sanskaar"* *and light the 'funeral pyre.' It* **was an emotionally traumatizing time for me, and I was in my late teens then.** Fortunately, our well-wishers helped me, **my mother (Bubbles)** and my sister **Shrishti** to cope with the tragic grief. With great difficulty I reconciled with this harsh reality and consoled myself thinking that 'nothing in life is permanent.' My all-time personal favorite RDB tracks include 'Jaane jaan' (Jawani Diwani) and 'Samandar mein nahaake' (Pukar). We will always remember Pancham-da for the gem of a human being that he was, and of course for his versatile range of chartbuster melodies.'

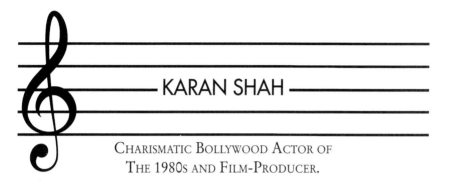

KARAN SHAH

CHARISMATIC BOLLYWOOD ACTOR OF
THE 1980S AND FILM-PRODUCER.

Today whatever screen identity I have is mostly due to chartbuster songs like 'Tu rutha toh main' (Jawani), which R. D. Burman composed for my debut film and also for successive movies including my home production 'Chor Pe Mor.' And of course, thanks to my mentor, the legendary film-maker, Ramesh Behl who launched me and Neelam together in 'Jawani.' **The fun-loving outspoken Pancham added a 'zing' to everyone's life including mine with his affable nature and extraordinary musical caliber. Being a hardcore foodie, he was extremely fond of my home-made Gujarati *kadhi* (curry), and whenever he was recording at Film Center, my mother used to prepare it and send.** We stayed in the vicinity of Wilson College, not far from Tardeo, where RDB's recordings took place. As a party-host, he would be the 'life' of the party, and I would be the official 'bartender' supervising the cocktails. At his music-sessions, **I had a blast because dada was fond of using abusive slang as 'dummy lyrics,' and lyricist Gulshan Bawra would be heard grousing. "*Yaar Pancham, aise gaali-galoch lafzon par main gaana kaise likhun.*" Gulshan-ji would crib, and RDB would give him an amused look.**

My personal favourite RDB track from 'Jawani' is 'Gali gali doonda tujhe.' But I admire the way he brilliantly arranged the fusion of sitar strummings in the 'Tu rootha toh' interlude, where he drifts far away from the main melody but gracefully returns to the original scale. **Actually, by default, the keyboard player tapped an extra 'synthesized' clap sound key, and RDB instantly said 'this pattern sounds better, let's retain this.' So that's how one hears the three clap sounds in the mukhda.** Not many people know that one of the songs which RDB had composed, **'Aaj ka daur' (Chor Pe Mor), was banned by All India Radio** because of certain lyrics (koi hai voton ka chor), which during the early 1990s the authorities felt was objectionable. In this same song I played the drums correctly on-screen for ninety seconds, and RDB complimented me and said *"superb, kamaal kar diya." We even had a song 'Ae ladki chaabi de dey'* in which stalwart actor Naseeruddin Shah had to recite racy dialogues while Asha-ji (Bhosle) sang. During the recording, I remember Asha-ji seemed to be blushing as she knew that a portion of the lyrics had a 'double meaning.' Until RDB, using his presence of mind, convinced her that since Naseer-bhai was playing a police officer, the song had to be decent. **Actually I consider myself very lucky that RDB has sung the magical number 'Toone kiya kya jaadoo' (Apne Apne), in his own voice. This high-octave complex RDB song was picturised on me** rollicking with my heroine Mandakini in the midst of a chilled waterfall in Kudremukh, where I am 'shirtless.' In order to match the intensity decibels of Pancham-da's vocals, **I had to belt it out in a loud volume during the shoot, and my jugular veins are visible. At the end of the shooting, I actually lost my voice. Only Rahul-da, I repeat only Rahul-da, could have sung this complex raga-based Western song.**

To sum up, all I can say is that RDB was extra-passionate about his music, but that unfortunately did not make him a 'businessman.' Somehow I feel he let himself be 'used' by others. When he needed them most during his low-days, almost all of them had deserted him, with the exception of a few close 'true loyal friends'.'

BHAVANA BALSAVER

POPULAR ACTRESS, DAUGHTER OF NOTED VETERAN
ACTRESS SHUBHA KHOTE AND KARAN SHAH'S WIFE

'People may think I am crazy, but honestly I have religiously watched movies such as 'Lava,' 'Sitamgar,' 'Manzil Manzil' and 'Jawaani' only because of RDB's fabulous music. I am one of his most ardent fans with unconditional loyalty. Even the divine force above realized how genuine my love for RDB's music is, which is why I guess I bagged the Marathi film 'Sukhi Sansarache 12 Sutre' produced by Satish Wagle and directed by Anil Baindur. It had all of its songs composed by Pancham-da. What mattered to me most was that RDB's name appeared as the 'music director.' The tragic part was that when the movie released, he had already passed away. Most of these Marathi songs are inspired from RDB's own popular Bengali or Hindi ones. Like for instance, 'Roon jhoon jhoon' has the flavour of the RDB Hindi track 'Gumsum tum hai sanam.' Although I never got to meet dada personally, this movie assignment was indirectly the biggest consolation for me.

Since **Mehmood uncle,** who shared a very warm rapport with RDB right from his initial days in Bollywood, also had a close professional rapport with my mother **Shubha Khote, my mom knew Pancham-da personally.**

There is a hilarious parody song from 'Laakhon Mein Ek' which has music by RDB. It is picturised on my mom and Ramesh Deo.'

'RDB imbibed the grand legacy and style of his great father Sachin Dev Burman. But he also maintained his own individual style using innovative contemporary rhythm. Four decades ago, Pancham-da's music had become a rage and it continues to do so even today. Every top film-maker wanted his (RDB) tunes. I stayed at Hotel Caesar's Palace for a while where RDB had his 'sittings.' I used to observe a bee-line of directors pacing up and down in the gallery and corridor, as his room was always 'house-full.' This was the phenomenal craze and demand for RDB's scores. My favorite RDB composition as a 'disco dance' number is 'Mehbooba mehbooba' (Sholay) and in the classical genre it's 'Chingari koi bhadke' as it gives me an emotional high.'

– **B. Subhash,**
Prolific producer-director of iconic retro-musical movies including 'Disco Dancer' and 'Tarzan,' both of which had Bappi-da's hit music scores.

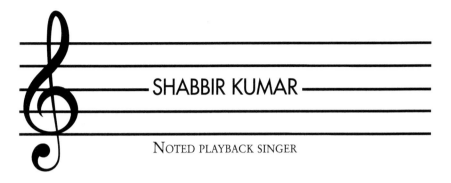

SHABBIR KUMAR

NOTED PLAYBACK SINGER

'Pancham ne di aawaz, aur lo main aa gaya'

'When I got a message at the modest guest house located at Mumbai Central, where I was staying, that the legendary R. D. Burman wanted me to come over for a 'sitting' of an upcoming big banner movie, it was as if a lightning bolt from the blue had struck me. Sometime later I got to know that it was for the movie 'Betaab' in which Sunny Deol was to be launched. Actually I was not new to music-biz as I had already recorded playback for all the songs in the iconic film 'Coolie.' And by the grace of God, I had lent my voice for superstar Amitabh Bachchan. Songs like 'Saari duniya ka bojh hum utthaate hain' were immensely popular. The credit for this goes to director Manmohan Desai and the composer duo Laxmikant-Pyarelal.

Frankly, singing for Pancham-da was a dream come true. Not many people are aware that I am not formally trained in music. So when I went to meet RDB, I honestly told him that I am a *'Kansen'* who had learnt music by diligently listening to songs and that I am definitely not a *'Tansen'*! Much to my surprise, the modest RDB laughed and said, 'Sometimes it's an advantage when singers are not classically trained, and I enjoy working with them.' This was a huge morale booster for me.

The critical test was when Pancham-da told me that I would be singing a duet with the legendary Lata-didi (Mangeshkar). The song was 'Jab hum jawaan honge.' And I was so awestruck with admiration for didi that when I stood at an arm's distance from her facing the mike for the first time in the singer's cabin, *meri bolti bandh ho gayi*! Just imagine, everytime when my turn came to sing, I was dumbstruck. This happened thrice because I was very jittery. Fearing the worst, I was mentally prepared to be scolded and sent home. Just then Lata-didi in her soft dulcet voice said, *"Pancham, chalo chhota-sa break lete hain."* Apparently she sensed what I was going through. Of course the boss agreed instantly. In the presence of RDB, she urged me to have tea and light snacks and began cheering me up to bring me into a comfort zone. Meanwhile, RDB came from behind and whispered in my ear, *"Shabbir apne aap ko suron ka sher samajh lo and give your best"* and patted my back.

The break got over and didi said, *"Chalo Pancham ab 'take' karte hain."* Honestly I don't know what happened because I was in seventh heaven, and I sang with complete confidence. I was impatient to know what RDB had to say. And he exclaimed 'superb, no need for any retakes.' After a few minutes, producer-actor Dharmendra-ji came and kissed my forehead and hugged me, followed by actor Sunny Deol who also complimented me. Although I was skeptical, knowing how unpredictable music-biz is, I was asked to come subsequently to record all the songs. What I observed was that RDB had reinvented his style for all the 'Betaab' songs. They were 'flowing' songs that one could enjoy humming and not the typical dance numbers.

It was pointed out to me by some music experts that for the 'metre' and 'tempo' Pancham had kept in mind the country-side ambience, and also that Sunny Deol was not the conventional agile dancer. The music of 'Betaab,' which emerged a superhit, figured in the Filmfare nominations for 'Best Music.' This proves that even when RDB deviated, the masses appreciated.'

'Although I have made many movies, the film 'Agar Tum Na Hote,' which I co-produced, is a musical milestone that I am proud of. And the credit goes to mahaan sangeetkar Pancham-da who put his heart and soul in composing its outstanding music. The lyrics of the mukhda of the title-song was a joint effort by Gulshan Bawra and Pancham. Even today, the title song 'Humein aur jeene ki,' which won legendary singer Kishore-da the Filmfare Award, with its fantastic 'fusion' of piano, accordion and sitar notes, is evergreen. Pancham-da was so sentimentally attached to this movie and its songs that he has given fabulous 'aalap' vocals in his own voice for the background score.

On the sets, we used to hear heroine Rekha constantly humming ghazals or some filmi number whenever she was not shooting. So we asked Pancham-da whether we could get Rekha to recite one of the duets, 'Kal Sunday ki chutti.' **Not only did RDB go out of the way to rehearse with Rekha but assured us that he would give us a catchy song which would help us in our publicity as well.** Then there was this sensuous song 'Dheere dheere zara zara' sung by Asha Bhosle. In this track **RDB, with his whacko ideas, got a bunch of keys for its sound effects in the** *mukhda* and for the rest of the song. During the 'sound mixing,' the technician goofed up, and the 'swishing-jingle' sound apparently got 'muted' in the rest of the song. **Being a perfectionist, RDB was very upset with this** *'galti'* when he heard the final optical track—but nothing could be done. **In the picturization of this song, Rekha has hooked an ornate bunch of keys onto her waist and keeps tapping on it to sync with the sound effect.** Besides producing 'ATNH,' I had the privilege of being an assistant to the noted film-maker J. Om Prakash for the landmark movie 'Aap Ki Kasam,' which was yet again a musical testimony to RDB's extraordinary caliber.'

– **Vimal Kumar**
Noted senior prolific Bollywood film-maker

'Actually all the movies I have directed are 'inspired' by R. D. Burman's music. In fact, I was the first person to 'use' Pancham-da's tunes as a romantic 'background' in my directorial debut movie 'Main Hoon Na.' Even the movie hero, Shah Rukh Khan, used to love RDB's serenading song tunes. When I was assigned by film-maker Vidhu Vinod Chopra to choreograph the iconic songs of '1942: A Love Story,' it was an honour and a turning point in my career. **Frankly speaking, I was so excited and ecstatic 'only' because it had R. D. Burman's music.** It did not matter to me, at that point of time, who else was in the cast or crew.'

– **Farah Khan**

Ace choreographer and maverick movie director

KUMAR SANU

ACCLAIMED PLAYBACK AND 'LIVE' CONCERT SINGER

'According to me, Pancham-da is the **best composer** because of his talent and futuristic vision. The fact that, even after four decades, his songs are so popular with today's 'WhatsApp age' youth. In 1993 when I went to Film Center for the song recording of '1942: A Love Story,' Rahul-da just gazed at me from top-to-toe and said, **'We can't record like this**—you have an unshaven look, disheveled hair, and not-so-impressive clothes.' I was bewildered because I could not figure out 'why' my external appearance mattered so much when it was just my throat and mouth which would indulge in the 'singing.' 'We will meet again, don't worry. This song will be sung by you and nobody else,' dada (RDB) assured me.

Disappointed, I made my exit that day, but on the rescheduled day I walked into Film Center as a different person—clean-shaven and clad in smart clothes. Dada immediately 'approved' of my persona and said, "*Aaj gaana theek record ho jayega, aur aage chalkar havoc bhi create karega.*" **Then he asked me to sing that repeat-simile word** '*jaise*' **in varying tones in the classic solo melody 'Ek ladki ko dekha toh'** '*Jaise*' is sung seven times in each refrain, and there is no 'antara.' After the final take was approved, I took the liberty to check with Pancham-da for the actual reason 'why' he did not record with me the previous time. Patiently dada explained to me that they had worked very hard on the 'challenging' songs for the past several weeks, and that he had conceived a 'vision' of a handsome, immaculate hero in his mind. So when he saw me the last time he got 'discomforting vibes,' which unsettled him. **This kind of commitment and dedication to creativity is what set RDB a class apart.'**

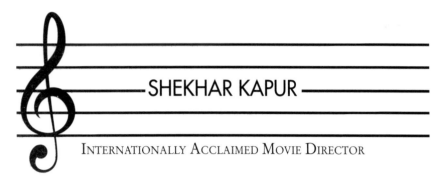

SHEKHAR KAPUR

INTERNATIONALLY ACCLAIMED MOVIE DIRECTOR

'What a masterpiece songs-score R D Burman came up with, for my directorial debut 'Masoom' (1982) which even won him the Filmfare Award. Although Panchamda had been working mainly with established big-time film-directors, he never made feel that I was new, from nowhere and knew nothing about film-making. On the contrary, Dada gave me and 'Masoom' the best of his creative attention—that resulted in an amazing set of sterling tracks. Since the dance-master was not available, I was inspired by the classy song 'Huzur Iss Kadar Bhi' and I managed to choreograph the party-mood dance movements.

Twelve years later, on Jan 3rd 1994, I was working on the background music of 'Bandit Queen,' of a mournful tragic scene, with composer-singer Nusrat Fateh Ali Khan in Lahore. That night, pre-dawn, we got the shocking news that RDB had passed away. The very next day, Nusrat-saab wished to pay his homage to Pancham-da. So moved was he, as he was very fond of him, that he wished to express his sorrow. Looking into my eyes, he sang on the mike, straight from his heart—a soulful vocal tribute for Panchamda. 'Use it wherever you wish in the movie,' the 'late' Khan-saab had then told me.'

Bichde sabhi baari baari...

'DOSTI SABHI NIBHAATE HAIN, LEKIN KOI
'SACHHA DOST' NAHIN HAIN' —PANCHAM

When I (the author) used to meet Pancham-da during 1992–93, his health seemed okay except for minor issues. But what was hurting him and led to depression was that slowly the Bollywood industry had 'disowned' him. Most music companies felt he was 'no-longer-saleable.' To whomsover he was close to, Pancham would grouse, *"Mujhe daam nahin, sirf kaam chahiye."* When I met him at Marylands, he even reacted to me with a tinge of anguish in his voice, *"Industry mein mooh-boli dosti sabhi nibhaate hai, lekin koi 'sachha dost' nahin hain."* Except for a few close 'loyal' friends like Randhir Kapoor, Rishi Kapoor, producer Barkha Roy, film-maker Vidhu Vinod Chopra, singers like Shailendra Singh, Sushma (Poornima) Shrestha, a few of his core team musicians and his manager Bharat Ashar, the rest of the Bollywood biradari seemed to have 'royally deserted' the melody king. It may sound uncanny that this real-life situation reminds one of the heart-rending lyrical lines 'Dekhi zamaane ki yaari... bichde sabhi baari baari,' coincidentally composed by his illustrious father S. D. Burman.

At the well-attended late-night premiere of the Jackie Shroff starrer 'Gardish' (1993), held at Novelty theatre (at Grant Road in central Mumbai), as an invitee, I soon realized that R. D. Burman was 'conspicuously missing.' There was a 'live' brass band playing outside the theatre. The band leader who was anxiously waiting to welcome his 'favourite' composer with a fanfare of trumpets was utterly disheartened when there was a 'no show' from RDB. Little did he know that RDB 'did not get his invitation' for the premiere. The maiden screening as well as the lavish after-party held at the Taj Palace, which I attended, was without the music director. Interestingly, the southern charismatic superstar Mohanlal was among the special VVIP invitees at the same party, as he had acted as the lead in the original Malayalam version titled 'Kireedam.'

It was very disturbing to see something like this happening to a music legend—a legend whose mesmerizing music was instrumental in scores of musical jubilee hits and in making overnight sensations out of so many debutant star-sons.

Recalls the outspoken Rishi Kapoor, 'Whenever I would call or meet Pancham-da to cheer him up, he would ask me about my upcoming movies with the hope that maybe I would 'recommend' his name as its composer. Had it been possible, I would have willingly done that. Unfortunately, all the new films that I signed already had some other music director finalized in advance. It used to be agonizing for me to be 'unable' to help Pancham-da to tide over his career crunching crisis. Being a creative workaholic, he desperately wanted to return to the recording studios.'

Singer Sushma (Poornima) Shrestha has tears welling in her eyes as she recollects her last few encounters with the music director. 'What I realized was that RDB was also longing for company to converse with. Whenever I went to his apartment during his slack phase, he would be so elated that he would compel me to sit, chat and have some food with him. You know he confided in me that he would occasionally ask some of his producer, director 'friends' to join him at a venue of their choice and give him company. But they would excuse themselves claiming that they 'had no time as they were too busy elsewhere.' Since he was quite sensitive, this 'loneliness' was apparently wreaking havoc on his well-being,' laments Poornima.

Eminent composer Anand (of the Anand-Milind musical duo) shudders when he vividly recalls excerpts from his scary conversation with RDB a few months before he passed away. 'It was at a private wedding reception at Juhu Hotel lawns where Pancham-da and I were sitting together in a corner, away from the gathering of guests. Whenever dada would call up his producer-friends, they would interrupt and say, 'Yaar I am so busy, let me call u back'—and they would never call back. RDB confided in me that he would sometimes ask some of his film fraternity 'friends' to join him for cocktails and dinner and even mention that 'he' would pick up the restaurant bill. Even then, they would not turn up. He said that he would often be standing 'all alone' in his balcony gazing at the traffic passing by. But what rattled me most was when he poured out his heart-wrenching sentiments to me, '**as my well-wisher, do pray that the period music of '1942: A Love Story' generates a huge hungama, which will be like a tight slap to the industry detractors. And only then I will leave this world.**' What was unnerving was that he mentioned this profound hard-hitting statement two or three times, as if he had some sort of premonition,' recollects Anand.

Producer Devi Dutt, (younger brother of Guru Dutt) who met RDB during his slack phase, recalls how RDB lamented that 'even after giving music for over 325 films, I have only one last film, '1942: A Love Story,' of producer Vidhu Vinod Chopra, who has promised me that he will continue giving me more films in the future. It's strange that I often remember and hear your brother Guru Dutt's hard-hitting song 'Dekhi zamane ki yaari, bichde sabhi baari baari.'' It was so distressing to hear RDB say all this that I warmly hugged him and assured him that his jinxed phase would soon come to an end.

Epilogue—Past Forward

Illustrious film-maker Mahesh Bhatt's candid 'take' on and touching tribute to R. D. Burman

No matter how great a human being is, most of them eventually end up with just a portrait on the wall of fame or maybe a bronze statue at some vantage public location. Some of them discreetly fade into oblivion. That's what makes composer-singer Rahul Dev Burman one of those gloriously glaring exceptions.

His unconventional legacy of awesome music itself is perpetual. He will always 'live' in the hearts of millions of Indians and NRIs, especially those who have a passion for retro film-music. With his path-breaking scores, most of them which 'jolt' you with their innovative streaks, the maverick man also dared to debunk the rigid idiom of the traditional stereotypes of song composing and background scores. Time is generous to genuine geniuses and unforgiving to fake ones.

As a fairly new 'film director,' I had the fortune and privilege to work with the well-established and popular RDB for a couple of my movies, **'Vishwasghaat' (1976) and 'Naya Daur' (1978)**. At the song-sessions, there was no grappling for tunes or any labored air around RDB—quality music came to him so easily. That I suppose is the sign of a 'great master.' Interestingly, in one of the 'Naya Daur' songs, which goes 'Paani ke badle pee kar sharaab,' RDB inserted that intriguing bottle-blowing sound effect *(similar to the one used in the prelude of the 'Sholay' song 'Mehbooba mehbooba')* which Rishi Kapoor and Danny have perfectly lip-synced on-screen.

There have been allegations that RDB was occasionally partially 'inspired' by Western tunes, 'refrains' of which he 'lifted and adroitly Indianized and blended' in some of his hit songs. With absolutely no malice meant towards anyone, let me state that, in general, the human brain is a recycling bin and cannot produce something out of nothing. All human brains are a sum total of whatever we have seen, heard or experienced in our lives. To claim that someone is a fountainhead of absolute originality could be deemed a delusion. All of us 'inhale' the works of great people during our lifetime, which in turn leaves an imprint on our consciousness—which tends to bleed into our work and often finds creative expression. **Everything in human culture is sourced or derived from something else. That's my candid take.**

There were two stages of Pancham-da's career during which I met him. The first was when he was at his peak—post his musical milestones such as 'Hare Rama Hare Krishna,' 'Sholay' and 'Khel Khel Mein.' The second time was when he was going through his vulnerable slack period between 1990 and 1993. In the latter phase, where I once saw him waiting at the 'T-Series' production office, he seemed to be in dire distress and desperately looking for that one swift curve that would restore his lost glory.

In success-centric showbiz, people generally disown even legends going through that 'no-longer-saleable' phase and then 'glorify' that same person soon after as he is 'no more.' Apparently, it's easier to 'deify' people who have departed from this world. A 'winner' is a loser who refuses to give up. And with his sterling scores of '1942: A Love Story,' composer R. D. Burman with his enduring brilliance emerged a 'winner.' Call it a brutal irony of fate that he was no longer around to witness his own return to supremacy amidst deafening applause, which is still reverberating.

As he makes his debut as an author, I extend my best wishes and blessings to Chaitanya Padukone, a dedicated, music-savvy senior showbiz journalist whom I have known since the days of my 1984 landmark film 'Saaransh.'

– MAHESH BHATT

Acknowledgements

My heartfelt, grateful **thanks to each honourable** celebrity,as listed below, most of whom are also my well-wishers, for extending their esteemed and timely co-operation in sharing their fond memories of / tributes to the **iconic R. D. Burman,** which are published in this book. Your proactive support meant a LOT to me, as this happens to be my 'debut' book.

I wish to express my special and earnest gratitude to Amitabh Bachchan-ji, Lata-Didi Mangeshkar, Asha Bhosle-ji, Randhir-ji and Rishi Kapoor, Sanjay Leela Bhansali, A. R. Rahman, Zeenat Aman, Sunil Gavaskar, Shyam Benegal, Ramesh Sippy, Hema Malini, Babul Supriyo, Ameen-bhai Sayani, Pyarelal-ji Anandji-bhai, Ashim Samanta, Raj Sippy, Goldie Behl, Leena Chandavarkar-Ganguly, Bhupinder Singh, Anup Jalota, Talat Aziz, Annu Kapoor, Hariharan, Anand-Milind, Vidya Balan, Shatrughan Sinha-ji, Suniel Shetty, Shekhar Kapur, Sonu Nigam, Himesh Reshammiya and Jackie Shroff.

The following **top-grade musicians** closely associated with **Panchamda** and who are/were also known to me on a personal level over the years offered me valuable inputs, insights, startling data and even images relating to their boss during my personal discussions with them, either at RDB's recordings during the 'lunch-break' or in the recent past at film events. My **heartfelt THANKS** to each one of them.

RDB's Team of Musicians

Kersi Lord, Burjor 'Buji' Lord, Uttam Singh, Amrutrao Katkar, Franco Vaz, Bhupinder Singh, Late Homi-da Mullan, Late Manohari-da Singh, Ramesh Iyer, Bhanu-da Gupta, Ranjit 'Kancha' Gazmer, Raju Singh, Viju A. Katkar and Nitin Shankar.

During my film-journalistic and creative writing career, the following people connected with the media or other vocations have directly or indirectly contributed as 'catalysts' to the steady progress in my career. Without their timely moral support, I could not have achieved what I have today. My earnest and grateful THANKS to each one of them *(in alphabetical order):*

Ashwin Thakkar, Ayaz Memon, Barkha Roy, Bharat Ashar, Bhawana Somaaya, Chunky Pandey, Camaal Mustafa Sikander, Devi Dutt, Farhana Farook, Fiona Fernandez, Freyan Bhathena, Heena S. Karekar, Hemal Ashar, Indranil Roy, Jitesh Pillaai, Jatin S. Wagle, K. Haridas Bhandary (statistical data analysis), Kaushal Punatar, Mohan Deep, Mohan Hemmadi, Nari Hira, Nitin Sethi, Namdeo M. Kuray (Pune), Pinki Virani, Pritam Sharma, Pradyuman Maheshwari, Prahlad Kakkar, Ram Jawhrani, Raj Nayak, Rajiv G. Rai, Sachin Pilgaonkar, Sarita A. Tanwar, Shailendra U. Kamdar, Shashikant Jadhav, Shubha Shetty-Saha, Subhash K. Jha, Suvarna Kagal-Ghaisas, Uday Shankar Pani, Umesh Chandra Malviya, Vishwas Nerurkar (statistical data records), Viral Bhayani.

THANKS A TON also to Abbas Hakim, Ajit Deval, Ajit Ghosh, Amod Mehra, Ananth Mahadevan, Anurag Pandey, Ashok Vashodia, Ashoke Shekhar, Atul Maru, Ajay Sheth, Aneel Murarka, Bharati Dubey, Bharathi S. Pradhan, Bimal Parekh, Bipin Pandit, Brahmanand Singh, Dale Bhagwagar, Darshini Shah, Deepa Gahlot, Dilip Sashital, Dilip Thakur, Gajanan Mestry, Harish Bhimani, Hemant Kenkre, Himanshu Jhunjhunwala, Hemlata Vinod Sharma, Jagdish Aurangabadkar, C. P. Joseph, Jyothi Venkatesh, Karan Shah, Komal Nahta, Kushal Gopalka, Kartik Tripathi, Lakshmi (Asha) Sirur, Mahendra Hathi, Mahesh Shah, Manohar Iyer, Mohit Shastry, Narendra Kusnur, Nita Bajpai, Nittin Keni, Parag Chhapekar, P.K. Bajaj, Parul Chawla, Pradeep Bandekar, Prof. Purnima Sharma, Radhika Mohan, Rajiv Vijayakar, Rajkumar Karnad, Raju Bharatan, Raman Maroo, Shankar Iyer, Shashank Zare, Subodh Salunke, Suhas Dharadhar, Santosh Bhingarde, Sunil Ullal,

Sushant Dhond, Sushil Kumar Agrawal, B. K. Tambe, *entire Team Panchammagic (Pune)*, Udita Jhunjhunwala, Umesh Sathe, Vinay P. Jain (panchamonline), Vinod Yennemadi, Viral Bhayani, Vishwanath Shirali, Yogen Shah and Yogesh Lakhani.

A note of special thanks to my wife, Shweta Padukone, for her kind, encouraging, crucial moral support for the past seven months, and to my daughters Apeksha and especially Malavika for the timely I.T.-centric support extended to me at all times, despite my demanding deadlines.

'Author's Choice

Playlist of unconventional 27 RDB composed melodies'

1. Ae khuda har faisla (Abdullah)
2. Aaj ki raat koi (Anamika)
3. Aayo kahaan sey (Buddah Mil Gaya)
4. Aisa samaa na hota (Zameen Aasmaan)
5. Ab ke saawan mein jee dare (Jaise Ko Taisa)
6. Chanda o chanda (Laakhon Mein Ek)
7. Chala jaata hoon kisi (Mere Jeevan Saathi)
8. Dekho O deewano (Hare Rama Hare Krishna)
9. Dil tera hai main bhi (Bombay to Goa)
10. Dil mein jo baatein hai (Joshila)
11. Hum bewafaa hargiz (Shalimar)
12. Jago sone waalon (Bhoot Bungla)
13. Jiss gali mein, tera ghar (Kati Patang)
14. Jeevan mein tu darna (Khote Sikkay)
15. Jab andhera hota hai (Raja Rani)
16. Jab chaaha yaara tumne (Zabardast)
17. Koi mar jaaye (Deewaar)
18. Koi mane yaa na mane (Adhikaar)
19. Kaahe ko bulaaya mujhe (Humshakal)
20. Kya nazaare kya sitaare (Jheel Ke Us Paar)
21. Meri pyaari Bindu (Padosan)
22. Mera naam hai Shabnam (Kati Patang)
23. Meethe bol bole (Kinara)
24. Nadiya se dariyaa (Namak Haraam)
25. Sharabi aankhen, gulabi chehra (Madhosh)
26. Tumne mujhe dekha (Teesri Manzil)
27. Woh phir nahin aate (Aap Ki Kasam)

Author's Bio

Chaitanya D. Padukone is an eminent senior Bollywood film and music-biz journalist over the past three decades and is the recipient of the K. A. Abbas Memorial gold medal and trophy, which was conferred on him for creative excellence in film journalism by mega-star Amitabh Bachchan. More recently, he was honoured with the prestigious Dadasaheb Phalke Academy Award (2012) for his outstanding contribution to showbiz journalism. An alumnus of Lala Lajpat Rai College of Commerce and post-graduate of Bombay College of Journalism, Chaitanya has opted

The Author at the R. D. Burman Memorial Chowk at Santacruz, Mumbai.

to make his literary debut by penning his memoirs on maverick music icon R D Burman (Pancham-da), with whom he shared a personal rapport for ten years, from 1983 up to end 1993. Besides chatting with RDB at film parties and movie premieres, music-savvy Chaitanya had the privilege of connecting with the legendary sangeetkaar RDB at his song and background recordings at Film Center. A former senior executive with HDFC Ltd, his passion is playing Bollywood songs on Western rhythm instruments.